STUDIES IN PHILOSOPHY

edited by
ROBERT NOZICK
PELLEGRINO UNIVERSITY PROFESSOR
 AT HARVARD UNIVERSITY

BETWEEN DEFLATIONISM & CORRESPONDENCE THEORY

Matthew McGrath

LONDON AND NEW YORK

First Published 2000 by
Garland Publishing Inc.

Published 2013 by Routledge
2 Park Square, Milton Park, Abingdon, Oxfordshire OX14 4RN
711 Third Avenue, New York, NY 10017

First issued in paperback 2014

Routledge is an imprint of the Taylor & Francis Group, an informa business

Copyright © 2000 by Matthew McGrath

All rights reserved. No part of this book may be reprinted or reproduced or utilized in any form or by any electronic, mechanical, or other means, now known or hereafter invented, including photocopying and recording, or in any information storage or retrieval system, without written permission from the publishers.

Library of Congress Cataloging-in-Publication Data is available from the Library of Congress.

ISBN 13: 978-1-138-86555-6 (pbk)
ISBN 13: 978-0-8153-3852-9 (hbk)

Table of Contents

Preface   vii

1. Realism about Propositions and Properties   1
   - I. Introduction   1
   - II. Ontological Commitment   4
   - III. Are Properties and Contents on a Par with Sakes and Average Persons?   9
   - IV. Ackerman's Triviality Charge   13
   - V. Properties and Concepts? Propositions and States of Affairs?   16

2. Deflationism Rejected, Weak Deflationism Presented   25

3. Questions for Weak Deflationism   41
   - I. Is Weak Deflationism Circular?   42
   - II. Why Shouldn't One Seek a Correspondence Theory of Propositional Truth?   44
   - III. Does Weak Deflationism Stumble on the Explanation of General Facts Involving Truth   46
   - IV. Does Weak Deflationism Have the Resources to Explain the Obviousness of Propositions Expressed by Instances of the Schema 'p' is true iff p?   51
   - V. Can the Weak Deflationist Answer the Standard Objection to Correspondence Theories that if Truth Consisted in Correspondence with the Facts, Knowing Something is True would Require an Absurd Comparison between Sentences (Utterances, Beliefs) and Facts?   52
   - VI. Is Weak Deflationism Incompatible with Non-Factualist Theories of Certain Areas of Declarative Discourse, e.g., Moral Discourse?   54
   - VII. Why Can't We Use Higher-Order Quantification to Formulate Deflationism about Propositional Truth as a Universalized Biconditional?   58

4. A Challenge from David Lewis ... 61
  I. First Part of the Challenge ... 64
  II. Second Part of the Challenge ... 75

5. Truthmaking ... 87
  I. Question 1: Does Pursuit of the Truthmaker Project Require Acceptance of a Correspondence Theory of Truth Rather than a Deflationist Theory? ... 88
  II. Question 2: Is There Good Reason to Think the Truthmaker Project will be Fruitful? ... 94
  III. Truthmaking without the Truthmaker Project ... 99

6. The Liar Paradox ... 101
  I. Illustrations of Supervenience ... 103
  II. Categorial Preliminaries ... 108
  III. An (Almost) General Account of Truth ... 110
  IV. A Dilemma? ... 127
  V. Comparison with Kripke's Account ... 129

Bibliography ... 135
Index ... 139

Preface

This dissertation was written at Brown University between 1996 and 1998. It represents the first stage of a larger project on the nature of truth, the childhood of the project, hopefully, and not merely its infancy. The project examines the two theories of truth that, as D.M. Armstrong remarks, compete for the allegiance of many an analytic philosopher: the *correspondence theory*, which states that a proposition is true if it corresponds to some fact in the world, and *deflationism*, which states that all there is to truth is given by the easy transitions between claims such as "The proposition that snow is white is true" and "Snow is white". The correspondence theory characterizes truth as an important quality connecting us with the world. Deflationism, in its simplest forms, treats the truth predicate as a mere device for increasing a language's expressive powers, a means for stating information that could not efficiently be stated otherwise.

This project began as an attempt to defend the correspondence theory of truth from its deflationist detractors, but it soon changed course to become a defense of a peculiar kind of deflationism, a "weak" deflationism that appeals more to correspondence theorists, no doubt, than to self-described deflationists. This is a poor way to win the support of either camp, though I am pleased to say that a few philosophers, albeit not many, have told me they count themselves Weak Deflationists. Although I am not wholly satisfied with the explanations and illustrations offered in chapters 2-6 (especially chapter 6 on the liar paradox), I, too, remain a Weak Deflationist. My most serious misgivings about the dissertation concern the introductory chapter, which as I now see it, pays insufficient attention of fictionalist theories of properties and propositions. In future work, I hope to make good on a distinction mentioned in footnote 2, added after the submission of the dissertation to Brown, between *talking as if* there were certain objects and *making as if* there were such objects. Having noted this lacuna, I am inclined to think that even if the sort of realism about propositions defended in the first chapter proves unworkable, the theory of truth proposed in subsequent chapters may be regarded as "correct" in a natural sense of the word. That is, if the theory is not literally true, then it is either metaphorically true or true according to the useful fiction of propositions. I would be pleased indeed if Weak Deflationism shared the status of the standard account of validity in terms of models.

Portions of several chapters are now published in revised form. An earlier version of chapters 2 and 3 is published in *Mind* as "Weak Deflationism," and portions of chapter 3 appear in *Mind* as "Reply to Kovach." Chapter 4 is published with minor changes in *The Australasian Journal of Philosophy* as "The Concrete Modal Realist Challenge to Platonism."

I would like to acknowledge many people for their help and support. My advisor, Ernest Sosa, read numerous versions of every chapter and provided me in each case with comments that altered the course of my thought. I would also like to thank Marian David, James Dreier, Gary Gates, Robert Howell, Jennifer Lackey, Adam Kovach, Jaegwon Kim, Jay Newhard, Baron Reed, and James Van Cleve. Most of all, I am grateful to Allyn McGrath, for her unwavering support and encouragement through three long years of writing and searching for a permanent academic position. This dissertation is dedicated to her.

CHAPTER 1

Realism about Propositions and Properties

I. Introduction

The account of truth presented in the chapters that follow takes truth, at the most basic level, to apply to propositions or contents, and *being true* of or exemplification, to hold between properties and things. This first chapter is devoted to a partial defense of realism about propositions and properties.

What sorts of entities are eligible for truth and falsity? Sentences, utterances, and beliefs come to mind. Let us focus on the case of beliefs. We may distinguish (at least[1]) two components to a belief, an attitude component—the believing—and a content component—what is believed. We use 'belief' itself in different ways, sometimes to pick out the state (type or token) of *believing that such and such*, sometimes to pick out the content of the state (type or token). We may say 'His belief that hot fudge is the safest sundae topping to request in a new restaurant led him to request it', in which 'his belief' presumably refers to a belief state token. And we may say 'The belief that the Earth orbits the Sun is incompatible with the belief that the Earth does not orbit the Sun', in which 'belief' is used to fix on a content rather than a belief type or token.

We rarely attribute truth to belief states (types or tokens), reserving that attribution for the contents of beliefs. We say, "What Dole believes is true," rather than "Dole's believing what he does (or that p) is true". In fact, when we attribute truth to belief states, or to sayings (oral and written), we think of the believing or saying as true by virtue of truth of what is said or what is believed, i.e., as true by virtue of the truth of the relevant content. This fact will be important in subsequent chapters.

---

[1] Fregean worries together with Russellian sympathies may require us to assert a third component in belief: ways of conceiving or "modes of presentation."

But what are contents? Are they genuine entities? Does our talk of contents commit us to recognizing them as genuine entities? Or is talk about contents—talk about *what* is said and *what* is believed—rather trumped-up talk about belief states (types and tokens)? We talk, often enough, of doing things for the *sake* of another person, for our own sakes, for the sake of humanity. We talk of appreciating works of art for their own sakes, of valuing pleasure or knowledge for its own sake. But is not this talk, at bottom, really just talk about doing things to benefit others, oneself, humanity, the nation? about valuing pleasure and knowledge intrinsically rather than as instruments to other goods? If so, why should we not follow suit with content-talk and conclude that talk about *what Dole believes* is, at bottom, just talk about Dole's believing that such-and-such?

In the face of these questions, there are three possible replies. The first is to concede that talk of contents does not commit one to genuine entities picked out by the sortal 'content'. The second is to cite a point of disanalogy between the sake case and the content case. The third is to reject the presupposed treatment of the sake case and to insist instead that sake-talk, as well as content-talk, commits us to entities namable by these sortals.

On its face, the sake case presents the most powerful of a family of objections charging the believer in contents with ontological profligacy. We must therefore keep in mind that other members of the family, *e.g.*, objections stemming from the case of "average persons," may not present precisely the same problems for content realism.

How does the believer in contents explain her thesis? Perhaps in this way: contents are the sorts of entities that are objects of attitudes such as belief and thought, as well as objects of speech acts such as asserting and commanding; they admit of either truth or falsity. This account has the virtue of not introducing into the very definition of content realism the esoteric language of 'abstract', 'causally impotent', 'simple', 'complex', 'constituent', and so on. It thus leaves room for substantial (and esoteric) debate among content realists about the nature of contents: Are contents linguistic entities? Are they concrete? Are they simples?—not to mention room for substantial debate about the nature of the various propositional attitudes: Is believing a three-place relation between agents, contents, and ways of thinking? Is believing naturalistically reducible? *etc.*

Compare the following characterization of realism about sakes. Sakes are the sorts of things that are possessed by objects of concern; they are things for which agents may act, for which events may occur, for which objects of concern are valued, enjoyed, *etc.* This rough account has the same structural virtues as the former. It allows room for debate about the nature and status of sakes. Are sakes linguistic entities? Are they concrete? Are they simples?—not to mention room for debate about whether having a sake is naturalistically reducible.

Our questions must be these: Should we take sake realism seriously? If not, then why should we take content realism seriously?

First note that the sake objection, if successful, may prove too much. Consider Strawsonian realism about persons: persons are entities that are subjects of both physical and psychological predicates. We might finesse this some to distinguish persons from other thinking creatures, perhaps with some assistance from Frankfurt's (1971) notion of second order volitions. Regardless, the danger of the sake objection is apparent. We must admit that there are persons. So our observation of structural similarities between sake realism and person realism should not lead us to discard the latter with the former. Sakes may stay or go, but persons must stay. So if the sake objection is to undermine content realism, we need to be told what it is about content realism that it shares with sake realism and *does not* share with person realism that makes it questionable.

What is so bothersome about sake realism? We may begin by noting that the truth of ordinary language sentences ostensibly about sakes, of ordinary sake-talk in general, is apparently fixed by the truth of sentences about non-sakes and their objects of concerns. 'Lois Lane risked her life for Clark Kent's sake', if true, is true owing to the truth of something of the order of 'Lois Lane wanted to benefit Clark Kent and attempted to do so by actions that put her life at risk'. Sakes, we might then think, would be supervenient entities. But if so, why worry about recognizing them? Tables, chairs, and perhaps even persons are supervenient entities, yet real. The opacity of 'sake' talk points us toward an answer to this question. Consider the following two sentences:

1. Lois Lane risked her life for Clark Kent's sake.

2. Lois Lane risked her life for Superman's sake

Suppose, as the story goes, that Lois Lane is ignorant of Clark Kent's true identity. Suppose, further, that (1) is true. Lois Lane, say, dodged bullets in an effort to reach Lex Luther's headquarters to dissuade him from taking Clark Kent's life. Is (2) true? No. Lois Lane did not think Superman's life was in jeopardy, and in fact hoped Superman would come to her protection. Examples like this show that to do something for a sake under one description does not entail do it for the same sake under another description.

If we took sake-talk to be reducible to talk of valuing and benefiting, (1) and (2) would become something like:

1'. Lois Lane wanted to benefit Clark Kent and attempted to do so by actions that put her life at risk.

2'. Lois Lane wanted to benefit Superman and attempted to do so by actions that put her life at risk.

Yet unlike (1') and (2'), (1) and (2) entail the existence of sakes. To accept (1) and (2) in addition to (1') and (2') would be to incur a commitment to entities some of our most fundamental relations to which are not *real* relations, but "intentional" relations which hold only relative to a description. The latter notion is indeed problematic. If there is a relation holding between x and y, it ought to hold between x and y however they are described. If definite descriptions D and D' apply to an object named by N, and the relation expressed by a predicate V holds between the referents of N

and N', then it would seem that from $\lceil V(N,N') \rceil$, we may infer both $\lceil V(D, N) \rceil$ and $\lceil V(D', N') \rceil$.

II. ONTOLOGICAL COMMITMENT

Sake-sentences, construed literally, incur ontological commitment that their paraphrases in terms of valuing and benefiting do not. This might sound puzzling. One may object: if we have a case of genuine paraphrase, it must be a case of identity of meaning and content, and so identity of ontological commitment. At this point, it may be helpful to take a few steps back and discuss of the role of paraphrase in ontological commitment. I begin with Joseph Melia (1995):

> The word 'paraphrase' is misleading. Intuitively, P is a paraphrase of Q if P means the same as Q. But paraphrases in this sense are useless for our purposes. How can P and Q have the same meaning whilst only one of them is committed to a certain type of entity? (1995, p. 224n)

Following Melia, we might say rather that (1') and (2') are paraphrases of (1) and (2) because they "have the same implications for the concrete part of the world"(1995, p. 224n). We might only modify Melia's account of paraphrase in ontology by saying that a sentence S_2 is a ontological paraphrase of a sentence S_1 iff

(i) S_1 is committed to whatever entities and types of entity S_2 is;
(ii) S_1 is committed to some entity or some type of entity S_2 is not;
(iii) S_1 obviously entails S_2;
(iv) the conjunction of S_2 and an existential statement specifying the commiments of S_1 not shared by S_2 is obviously and necessarily equivalent to S_2;
(v) the additional commitments S_1 incurs are problematic.

This account, unlike Melia's, allows for the possibility of paraphrase of number-sentences into set-sentences. It also, felicitously, makes the answer to the question of whether one sentence is a paraphrase of another depend on the relative ontological insecurity of the sentence paraphrased.

Our account of paraphrase enables us, as it does Melia, to answer Crispin Wright's (1983) criticism of ontological reduction by paraphrase, a criticism that nicely brings to light and sharpens the intuitive puzzle mentioned earlier. In a discussion of proposed ontological reductions formulated as biconditional schemata, the right-hand sides of instances of which are the reducing sentences, Wright tells us:

> In fact, there is a kind of double-think going on. For when we are tempted to accept the reductionist's refinement, it is because we are accepting surface-grammatical criteria for whether or not the sentences on the right-hand sides involve reference to a certain sort of object. But if we are content to rely on surface grammar here, why not on the left-hand sides also? Yet we cannot rely on surface grammar on both sides: otherwise, by the plausible intuition sketched [that the reducing sentence translate the sentence reduced (1983, p. 30)], we should be forced to reject the equivalences. (1983, p. 32).

We answer Wright by denying *both* requirements, the translation requirement *and* the biconditional requirement. Admittedly, there are intimate connections between what reduces and what is reduced, but the connections are mediated by sentences expressing the additional ontological commitments of what is reduced. In our examples (1) - (2'), the philosopher wishing to reduce or paraphrase sake-talk will deny the material equivalence of (1) and (1') (of (2) and (2')). The sake-sentences (1) and (2) are committed to sakes, and so are strictly speaking false, but (1') and (2') are true. However, if (1') is conjoined with a sentence specifying the additional commitments of (1)—the sentence 'There is an entity that is unique sake of Clark Kent'—there is an obvious and necessary equivalence. Consequently, if we reject sakes, we must regard sake-sentences such as (1) and (2) as strictly false. Nonetheless, such sentences may have a good deal of truth in them, since they may entail strictly true sentences about valuing and benefiting. The practical value of sake-sentences, moreover, may outweigh the disvalue of being strictly false, for sake-talk gives us a simpler, more efficient means of capturing truths about valuing and benefiting. In this way, an error-theory of sake-talk is less radical than a Mackie-style error-theory of ethical language. If Mackie (1977) is right, there is little truth, if any, captured in asserting 'Stealing is wrong'. The speaker's audience learns an important truth by witnessing such a speech act, *viz.* that the speaker believes that stealing is wrong, but the falsehood expressed by the speaker contains little, if any, elements of truth.

We thus answer Wright by maintaining that, in identifying the ontological commitments of a sentence, we track the presence of singular terms. But what are the conditions being a singular term? As a start we may say that what passes the relevant broadly syntactic tests for being a singular term *is a singular term*. (We put aside for now the question of the status of the test: Is it definitive of 'being a singular term' or merely a criterial but non-definitional guide for identifying singular terms?) Delineating the right syntax for singular terms, however, is a difficult task. Dummett (1973, chapter 4) makes a good start with these criteria:

t is a singular term iff

(1) for any sentence $A(t)$, the inference from $A(t)$ to ⌈there is something such that $A(it)$⌉ is valid.
(2) for any sentences $A(t)$ and $B(t)$, the inference from $A(t)$, $B(t)$ to ⌈there is something such that $A(it)$ and $B(it)$⌉ is valid.
(3) For any sentences $A(t)$ and $B(t)$, the inference from ⌈it is true of t that $A(it)$ or $B(it)$⌉ to ⌈$A(t)$ or $B(t)$⌉ is valid.

These criteria suffer from two defects. First, they are at best criteria only for English singular terms. Second, they are jointly insufficient, as Dummett himself points out, even as criteria for English singular terms. Hale (1987) brings this out clearly, using Dummett's own example:

In particular, while [these conditions] exclude indefinite noun phrases such as 'a policeman' when they occur in grammatical subject or object position, they fail to exclude such phrases when they figure as grammatical complements. Thus from 'George is a policeman' and 'Henry is not a policeman' we may validly infer 'George is something which Henry isn't. (Hale 1987, p. 16)

Dummett's guiding thought is that singular terms are distinguished by their susceptibility to first-order objectual quantification. What he needs, then, is a way of distinguishing first-order from higher-order generality. Dummett proposes the following test: if 'something' expresses higher-order generality, demands for further specification will eventually terminate in an improper yet grammatically well-formed demand. Thus, in the case of 'George is something which Henry isn't', we may ask "Which thing is that?" and the answer will be "A policeman;" if we then ask "Which policeman?" our question will be well-formed and yet improper. Hale (1987, p. 17) cites the occurrence of 'something' in opaque contexts as problematic for this new criterion: in 'Edward believes that someone is leaking official secrets', 'someone' expresses first-order generality and yet the question, 'who is that?', while well-formed, may be improper.

I think we may circumvent Hale s worries if we substitute for Dummett's criteria the following:

t is a singular term iff

For a broad range of non-fictional *A*, the inference from $A(t)$ to [there is something such that $A(it)$ and it exists, namely *t*] is valid.

(We require, of course, that *A* and *t* be unambiguous in their occurrences.) This criterion, unlike Dummett s, connects *being a singular term* with 'exists'. It rules out, as desired, 'something', 'nothing', 'red'. (Either 'red' or the pronoun 'it' would need to be used ambiguously to guarantee, *e.g.*, the validity of the inference from 'The apple is red' to 'There is something such that apple is it and it exists, namely red'.) Consider now the example of George the policeman. From 'George is a policeman', we may not infer 'There is something such that George is it and it exists, namely a policeman'. If 'it' and 'a policeman' are used unambiguously, what is inferred uses a pronoun, unintelligibly, in both predicate position and singular term position. Note that we do not *use* the notion of a referentially transparent context in specifying the range of *A*. We simply require that the range be broad and non-fictional. This is enough to give us a guide to which are the singular terms of English and which are

---

[2] Does this account dictate that 'justice' is a singular term? And what of 'the average person', 'the way the Houston skyline looks', 'that Texas grapefruits are delicious', 'how to marry a multi-millionaire'? Admittedly, the test does not give us robust results. However, I think it is plausible to maintain that these do pass the test, for it is their passing tests like this that makes them, and the familiar sentences in which they occur, so ontologically troubling. Talk of 'the average person' is talk *as if* there is something that is the average person, some existent object. It is not *making as if* there is such an object, where *making as if* is something like *pretending*, which requires some appropriate psychology. But *talking as if* and *making as if* must be distinguished. I don't *make as if* there is such a thing as the average person, but I do *talk as if* there is. Note once again that this criterion for being a singular term is *not* put forth as an account of what it is to be a singular term, but merely as a test.

not.[2] We might go on to broaden our criteria to apply to singular terms in other languages by specifying that what is inferable from $A(t)$ is translatable into English in the appropriate way. Thus, we have:

t is a singular term of language L iff, where t in L is translatable into English as u

for a broad range of non-fictional A, where $A(...)$ is translatable into English as $T(...)$ the inference from $A(t)$ to a sentence of L that is translatable as ⌈there is something such that T(it) and it exists, namely u⌉ is valid.

While this condition is no longer a criterion merely for English, it still builds in a relativity to English, but I think it will suffice for our purposes.

Given this criterion for singular terms, one may and should ask: why should ontological commitment track the presence of singular terms? One answer—the answer Wright approvingly finds in Frege—is that the notion of an object is to be understood in terms of the notion of a singular term, the latter being understood syntactically, as defined by criteria such as the above. What it is to be an object, under this view, is to be eligible for being the reference (the semantic value) of a singular term. As for the notion of a property (Fregean concept), we have: what it is to be a property is to be eligible for being the reference (the semantic value) of a predicate. Ontological distinctions are explained in terms of syntactic ones. Wright (1983, p.14) claims this "syntactical priority thesis"expresses the core meaning of Frege's famous but elusive dictum 'Only in the context of a sentence does a word have any meaning'.

The Fregean accounts of object and property confront the well-known paradox of the property (concept) *horse*. The accounts just discussed of objecthood and propertyhood leave open the question of whether these categories overlap. But a natural criterion for sameness of reference—intersubstitutability in extensional contexts *salve veritate*—decides the matter in the negative. 'is a horse' and 'the concept *horse*' cannot meaningfully be substituted for one another, and so are not intersubstitutable in extensional contexts *salve veritate*. This criterion, together with the truism that an expression of the form 'the F that is G' refers, if at all, to an F, give us the paradox: the expression 'the property *horse*' is a referring singular term; what it refers to is a property, *viz.* the property *horse*; so the property *horse* is not a property, since it is the referent of a singular term.

To solve the paradox, one must either reject either (i) the criterion for sameness of reference, (ii) the truism concerning the reference of definite descriptions, or (iii) the Fregean accounts of what it is to be an object, a property. I reject (iii). If something exists and we know about it, it is a possible object of reference by means of a singular term. 'The property horse' refers to the property horse. What of the predicate 'is a horse', then? I think we do best to say that predicates express properties while property-designators of the form 'The property F' or 'F-ness' refer to them. What the predicate 'is a horse' expresses is one and the same thing as what the singular term 'the property *horse*' refers to. Expression of a property is then explained in terms of mental attribution, attribution in thought. Thus, 'is a horse' expresses the property *horse* insofar as the predicate is usable, given the conventions of English, to attribute the property *horse* to things. Reference to an object is explained correspondingly: 'the property *horse*' refers to the property *horse* insofar as the singular term is usable, given the conventions of English, to attribute things to the property *horse*. Thus, we have a kind of attributional priority thesis: to be a property is to be eligible for being attributed to other things; to be an object is to be eligible for being the object of an attribution.

Given the attributional priority approach, we may explain the asserted connection between the use of singular terms and ontological commitment. Singular terms, by definition, are those that *aim* to refer. A term t aims to refer iff it is usable, given the conventions of the language, to attempt to introduce an object of attribution. The link between *being a singular term* and the criterion given for detecting singular terms is then this: a term t is usable, given the conventions of the language, to attempt to introduce an object of attribution iff t meets the syntactical criterion given for being a singular term. Why should this be? Because the occurrences within a sentence $A(t)$ of any t that satisfies the criterion are subject to first-order objectual quantification, and such quantification is used to express beliefs about what there is. If the truth of the belief expressible by asserting $A(t)$—for appropriate A—guarantees the truth of the existential belief expressible by asserting [Something is such that A(it) and it exists, namely t] , then t is an instrument of attempted reference.

What, then, is ontological commitment? If explicit criteria are desired, we might give several alternative sets of criteria, appropriate for different members of the family of notions of ontological commitment. Thus, for the broadest notion of the family, we might say:

> Sentence S (relative to L) commits person P to O = df P accepts S in knowledge of its meaning (in L) and the proposition S expresses (in L) metaphysically necessitates the proposition with respect to O that it exists.

> Sentence S (relative to L) commits person P to Gs = df P accepts S in knowledge of its meaning (in L) and the proposition S expresses (in L) metaphysically necessitates the proposition that Gs exist.

However, we might want a narrower conception of ontological commitment to explain how, although Berkeley commits himself to trees by asserting 'Trees exist', he does not commit himself to material objects. (I assume trees are material objects as a matter of metaphysical necessity.) The needed conception of ontological commitment must allow Berkeley's material object-beliefs—beliefs of the form *material objects are F*—to affect the commitments he incurs by asserting 'Trees exists'. The following seems to give us what we need:

> Sentence S (relative to L) commits person P to O = df P accepts S in knowledge of its meaning (in L) and the proposition S expresses (in L), in conjunction with P's non-controversial beliefs about what O would be if it existed entails in a narrowly logical sense that O exists.

Sentence S (relative to L) commits person P to Gs = df P accepts S in knowledge of its meaning (in L) and what S expresses (in L), in conjunction with one's P's non-controversial beliefs about the conditions for being a G, entails (in a narrow logical sense) that Gs exist.

Thus, although Berkeley commits himself to trees by saying 'Trees exist', he does not commit himself to material objects, since his relevant material object-beliefs do not connect with his belief that trees exist. He does not believe, *e.g.*, that if there are trees, trees are material objects. I include the adjective 'non-controversial' to prevent the consequence, for example, that Leibniz commits himself to monads in asserting 'There is a tree out the window'. Without the restriction, our definition would license the reasoning that, because Leibniz believes that if there is a tree, the tree is composed of monads, by his assertion of 'There is a tree out the window', he ontologically commits himself to monads. The insertion of 'non-controversial' clearly makes this notion of ontological commitment defined rather pragmatic, and perhaps, properly speaking, only relative to a population at a time.

A still narrower notion might forgo the connection with non-controversial beliefs:

Sentence S (relative to L) commits person P to O = df P accepts S in knowledge of its meaning (in L) and the proposition S expresses (in L) narrowly logically entails the proposition with respect to O that it exists.

Sentence S (relative to L) commits person P to Gs = df P accepts S in knowledge of its meaning (in L) and the proposition S expresses (in L) narrowly logically entails the proposition that Gs exist.

Further notions are obtainable by varying the strength of the necessitation relation possibly in conjunction with alteration of, or supplementation with, epistemic or doxastic conditions.

What is essential to all notions of ontological commitment is the connection to existential propositions. An existential sentence of the form 'There are Fs' commits one to Fs just because it states that there are Fs. A sentence containing a singular term 'the F that is G', *e.g.*, 'The F that is G is H' commits one to Fs insofar as what it expresses entails that there is at least (and also at most) one F. A sentence containing a name 'a' commits one to Fs, if it does, insofar as what it expresses, together with one's non-controversial belief that if a exists, a is F, entails that there are Fs.

III. ARE PROPERTIES AND CONTENTS ON A PAR WITH SAKES AND AVERAGE PERSONS?

Returning, then, to sake realism. The opacity of sake-talk makes sake realism objectionable. But it is objectionable for reasons of a more general relevance. By accepting sakes, we would confront a panoply of seemingly unanswerable questions: Do all things have sakes? My socks? The number 7? Do sakes themselves have sakes? Why is it that the things that have sakes have only one sake? Do things' sakes pre-date them, outlast them? Could things have had different sakes than they have? Why should we think that things have one and the same sake over time rather than that they enjoy different sakes at different times?

In trying to answer these questions, the sake realist turns to his supervenience base, truths about non-sakes valuing and benefiting. But reflections on the base provide little grounds for answers. Debates about the nature and status of sakes among sake realists would be idle.

Here lies a point of contrast with the case of persons. Difficult questions arise about persons, but we can make some headway in seeking answers. We have some grip on what sorts of things persons are. Persons are in space and time; persons have both mental and physical attributes; persons, like tables and chairs, exist and change over time.

The sake objection is not compelling in part owing to the referential opacity of sake-talk. What might be called the average person objection, however, does not share this shortcoming. This objection has it that because we are loath to believe there are such entities as average persons, we ought to have the same attitude toward contents. 'The average person is between 5' and 6' tall' is not referentially opaque. However, the second sort of objection we mentioned regarding sakes applies here *mutatis mutandis*. We do not understand how there could be such a thing as the average person. The average person would seem to be a person, but identical with no flesh-and-blood person we might find in space-time. The average person would have some fully determinate properties, but also would be indeterminate in certain ways: the average person would have a determinate height and weight, for example, but not have a determinate eye color, nor a determinate place of birth. The average person, mysteriously, would say 'I love you' to someone or other 3.7 (or some such) times per week, would attend church 2.3 (or some such) times per month, and would have 1.4 (or some such) siblings. The average person, unlike other persons, would have its characteristics determined by facts about the totality of persons. One is even led to absurd conclusions by accepting the existence of the average person: the average person is not identical to any particular person in the universe; so the average person isn't a person, but surely 'The average person is a person' is true, and so the average person would have to be a person. Identity of the average person over time is no less a morass. How could we answer the question whether the entity that is the average person in 1990 is one and the same as the entity that is the average person in 1997?

Furthermore, the obvious link between sentences such as (3) and (4) would invite eliminativism about average persons:

(3) The average person is between 5' and 6' tall.

(4) Persons, on average, are between 5' and 6' tall.

Relative to the assumption that there are average persons, the truth or falsity of (3) is determined by the truth or falsity of (4). Average persons, if there were such things, would be supervenient entities whose knowable, non-esoteric properties would be determined by the properties of persons according to simple schemes. Not only that, but the supervenience would be symmetrical: the average person exists, necessarily, iff there is at least one person; the average person is between 5' and 6' tall, necessarily, iff persons, on average, are between 5' and 6' tall; the average person likes chocolate, necessarily, iff persons, on average, like chocolate; and so on. Admittedly, there is no simple rule for eliminating the term 'average' altogether in contexts of the form 'The average person is F' in favor of talk about persons and numbers. If there were, average-person-talk would not be as useful as it is. Nonetheless, confronted with any piece of non-esoteric average-person talk, we can provide conditions that, relative to the assumption that there are average persons, are necessarily coextensive conditions about persons and numbers. We lose little truth in substituting the average-person-"free"talk for average person-talk. Both average person- and sake-talk buy us truth we can obtain without them, without their troublesome additional ontological commitments.

In sum, then, our ignorance of what average persons would be combined with our confidence that if there were average persons, knowable, non-esoteric average-person truths such as (3) would be involved in obvious and simple two-way supervenience connections to average-person-free sentences such as (4), together render average person realism highly unattractive.

Returning, then, to contents. Our questions must be these: Given the existence of contents, would non-esoteric content-truths be supervenient, in a fairly obvious and simple way, upon (relatively) unproblematic content-free truths? How firm is our grasp of what the nature and status of contents would be?

First, supervenience. One kind of test case concerns truths about persons' having propositional attitudes toward contents. Consider, for example, (5)

(5) Dole believes that everything Clinton said about him in his speech in San Francisco is false.

Suppose Dole does not know precisely what Clinton said about him in this speech but trusts his advisors that everything said was false. What content-free truths could determine (5), if it were true? This is a difficult question; it seems that if non-esoteric truths such as (5) are determined by content-free truths, the determination is neither obvious nor simple.

Moreover, non-esoteric content-truths would plainly not invariably be involved in two-way supervenience connections. The content that something Clinton said is true would be determined in one world by the fact that Clinton truly said that Ted Kennedy is a conservative and in another world by the fact that Clinton truly said that Bob Dole is a liberal.

Let us turn, then, to the question of our grasp of what contents would be. I assume that we have a firm (if incomplete) grasp of propositional attitudes, of belief, desire, *etc.,* of truth and falsity, and of relations of entailment, *bringing about, making probable*. We thus have a grasp of certain key relations contents would stand in, to one another and to items in the world, including ourselves.

However, we must confront questions about contents: Would contents be abstract? What would be their individuation conditions? And importantly: why would facts about the truth of contents correlate with content-free facts? Why would there be, *e.g.*, a necessary connection between the truth of the content that snow is white and snow's being white? The last questions, I think, are the most worrisome. But a few words about the former. Contents, we can be sure, would not be physical objects, and would not occupy space. Regarding individuation conditions, we believe that there are persons and that there are artifacts, but we struggle to give individuation conditions: Could there be two persons, two artifacts, having the same spatio-temporal worm? This is not to dismiss the difficult questions of whether, *e.g.*, <Hesperus is pretty>[3] *is* <Phosphorus is pretty> or <Catsup is tasty> *is* <Ketchup is tasty>. But it is not as if we lack a guide to such questions. Our guide is our body of knowledge, commonsense and reflective knowledge, regarding belief/desire psychology, semantics, and pragmatics. If, as Stephen Schiffer has argued, one cannot provide an adequate semantics for either natural languages or for the language of thought without invoking propositions, then the repudiation of propositions is costly.[4]

Contents, however, would be distinguished from persons and artifacts in their necessary satisfaction of equivalences of the form (T):

(T) The content that p is true iff p.

(The necessary satisfaction holds at least if we restrict our consideration to contents that do not involve truth or falsity). Why should facts about certain abstracta correlate necessarily with facts about concreta? It provides some relief to the content realist that set realists are faced with a parallel question concerning the necessity of instances of schema (S)

(S) x is a member of $\{x\}$.

If singletons, as sets, are abstracta, why should they stand in necessary membership connections to concreta?

The admission of unexplained necessary connections, though not unique to content realism, is undeniably a mark against it. But I submit that the case against contents is not decisive. Non-esoteric content-truths would not be invariably involved in two-way supervenience connections, let alone obvious and simple ones, and we have a relatively firm grasp of the sorts of relations contents would stand in. Crucially, the content realist may yet put to rest the most serious of objections to her account if she is able to explain the necessary connections of type (T). Moreover, if the (T) connections are explained and shown to be knowable *a priori* to anyone possessed of the involved concepts, knowledge of truth/falsity of contents may also be explainable. These considerations free content realists from the embarrassment attaching to sake realism and average person realism. Content realism may fail, but it cannot be dismissed as easily as average person realism or sake realism.

I give a similar partial defense of property realism. We are ostensibly committed to properties by our use of sentences containing singular terms such as 'redness',

---

[3] I follow Horwich (1990, p. 7) in abbreviating 'the proposition that p' by '<p>'.
[4] See Schiffer (1994, pp. 279-80).

'temperature', *etc.*; property-truths would not be invariably involved in two-way supervenience connections; and we have a relatively firm grasp of the key relations they would stand it. As with content-realism, however, property-realism is committed to troubling necessary connections:

(P) The property *F*-ness is exemplified by x iff x is F.

But I submit that this disadvantage to property realism does not obviously outweigh its advantages. The property realist, moreover, may hold out for an explanation of these connections in her account of exemplification, and then appeal to the *a priori* and obvious status of these connections, for those who have the involved concepts, to explain our knowledge of facts about *being true of* (exemplification) and facts about *being false of* (falsification).

IV. ACKERMAN'S TRIVIALITY CHARGE

A potentially more damaging objection to realism about contents and realism about properties argues that the purported distinctions between contents and non-contents and between properties and non-properties are not objective. Felicia Ackerman (1995) raises this objection forcefully concerning the property/individual distinction. She distinguishes two kinds of ontological questions, ontological-basics questions and ontological-status questions. Questions of both kinds are ontological, having to do with "what there is." We are not told outright wherein lies their difference, but Ackerman illustrates her distinction through examples. She writes:

> Consider a philosophy professor who is wondering
>
> (1) Will any of the students in my seminar have brown eyes?
>
> This sentence can be taken in more than one way. The first way is to take it as
>
> (2) Will any of the students in my seminar be brown-eyed?
>
> where (2) is indifferent to the ontological status of eyes but is to be answered affirmatively just in case not every student in question is either eyeless, or blue-eyed, green, hazel-eyed, etc. On the second construal, however, (1) asks a question that is different from (2) and receives an affirmative answer iff the empirical conditions necessary for an affirmative answer to (2) are satisfied *and* eyes have the ontological status of being entities. I will call questions of the sort expressed by (2) "ontological-basics questions" and questions of the sort expressed by (1), on the second construal, "ontological-status questions." (1995, p. 264)

Ackerman further illustrates her distinction by describing a "technique," which she says can be applied generally to "make whatever entity one likes the only entity in the world and turn "everything else" into properties of it" (1995, p. 265). Thus, for 'John and Mary are talking', Ackerman substitutes 'The number 3 John-Mary-talks', adding by way of explanation of the latter that is, the number 3 is such that John and Mary are talking, and neither John, Mary, nor the conversation is construed as an entity. (1995, p. 266)

(By 'entity', she means *individual that is not a property*.) Presumably, Ackerman conceives of 'The number 3 John-Mary-talks' as an answer to the ontological-status question 'Does the number 3 John-Mary-talk?' (It is convenient to use 'answer' in a way that does not imply that all answers are correct.) It is not clear to me whether she thinks 'Are John and Mary talking?' is a basics or status question, or correspondingly, whether she thinks 'John and Mary are talking' is a basics or status answer. Presumably, she would say that it depends on how one is *taking* these sentences. The following, admittedly rather imprecise, schematic rules for interpretation of "ways of taking" seem to justify Ackerman's statements:

(Rule 1) One takes an ordinary English sentence to treat N (Ns) as a *property* (properties) iff, one would accept as an ontological construction of it some English sentence (or perhaps some sentence of an extension of English) in which one of the following holds:

(i) 'N' figures as a constituent part of a non-relational predicate;

(ii) A predicate derivable from 'N' figures as a predicate or constituent of a predicate.

(Rule 2) One takes an ordinary English sentence to treat N (Ns) as an entity (entities) iff, one takes it not to treat N (Ns) as a property (properties) and one would accept as an ontological construction of it some English sentence (or perhaps some sentence of an extension of English) in which 'N' figures as a singular term (common noun).

A sentence S is an ontological construction of sentence S^*, roughly, if S makes explicit the ontology implicit in S^*. Ontology is made explicit with the use of singular terms and predicates: the use of a singular term (predicate) shows commitment to an entity (property). (Here I am only attempting to clarify Ackerman's conception of ontological commitment; I am not endorsing that conception.)

Consider Ackerman's example of 'John and Mary are talking'. One takes this to treat John as an entity if one would accept this sentence itself as making explicit its ontology. One takes it to treat John as a property if one would accept 'The number 3 John-Mary-talks' as making explicit the ontology. Grammar becomes somewhat difficult when we turn to the case of the philosophy professor wondering about the eye color of his students. We can say this: the professor understands 'I have a student with brown eyes' as treating eyes as entities if he would accept that sentence itself as making explicit its ontology; and he understands the sentence to treat eyes as a property (as properties?) if he would accept 'I have a brown-eyed student' as an adequate construction.

Ackerman's claim is that, not only can sentences such as 'John and Mary are talking' be construed as treating John as an entity or treating him as a property, but the two treatments are equally reasonable. The ontological-status claims expressed by 'John and Mary are talking', which treats John as an entity, and 'The number 3 John-Mary-talks', which treats John as a property, are both determined by the ontological-basic fact that John and Mary are talking. Ontological-status facts that differ in which things are therein counted as entities (properties) trivially supervene on ontological-basics facts. Matters of ontological status, then, are trifling: one may accept whichever things one chooses as entities or as properties, but there is no objective matter of fact that decides in favor of one choice rather than another.

I think Ackerman draws an improper inference. She infers the non-objectivity of the entity/property distinction from the existence and acceptability of easy transformations from ontological-basics sentences to a wide variety of ontological-status sentences (1995, p. 271). However, working with our rough definition of 'property' as *a thing which may be attributed to, believed of, true or false of other things*, if we think there are properties at all, we may assure ourselves that no person is a property. Neither John, eyes, nor the number 3 is a property, for they cannot be attributed to, believed of, or true or false of other things. We may attribute *being John* of something, but we cannot attribute John himself. *Being John*, if there is such a thing, is distinct from John, though John may be a constituent of *being John*, if *being John* is a Russellian property, *i.e.*, if it is a complex having a concrete constituent. Similarly, we can attribute *being blue-eyed*, but not eyes, *being the number 3*, but not the number 3.

The entity/property distinction, then, is objective in this sense: for any thing, there is a fact of the matter about whether it is an entity or a property. Moreover, there are reliable procedures, even if they are not statable in a set of simple rules, for judging entity and property candidacy: if there is such a thing as the number 3, it is an entity; if there is such a thing as wisdom, it is a property; if there is such a thing as *being such that John-Mary-talks*, it is a property. However, such objectivity is compatible with the non-objectivity of claims about the existence of entity-or property-candidates. So, although we know that *if* there is such a thing as the number 3, it is an entity, we might forever remain in the dark about whether there in fact is such a thing; perhaps there is even no right answer to be had at all.

Yet if we think that there are properties, things that can be attributed, *etc.*, then surely wisdom, *being blue-eyed*, *being John* are among them. And if we think there are entities, things to which we may attribute properties but which are not themselves properties, then surely Bill Clinton, John and Mary, and eyes are among them. I would even say that if there are entities, there are numbers. (By saying this, I am not committing myself to believing that numbers are *sui generis*; numbers might turn out to be sets or properties.) This is to say that the definition I provide for 'property' and 'individual' encourages latitudinarianism about properties and individuals. Still, this is not "anything goes" latitudinarianism. One cannot attribute anything to round squares, for there are none, as a matter of necessity. Nor, I submit, can one attribute anything to Hamlet, Othello, *etc*. Fictional persons do not exist and so are not potential subjects for attribution. Following David Lewis, I claim that when one "says something about Hamlet,"there is no person one describes; rather, one describes how things would be in a suitable world in which events of the kinds related in Shakespeare's play are realized. Moreover, property realism leaves room for debate about whether, for example, there are waves, smiles, snowballs, silences, causings, *etc.* That we apparently attribute properties by using sentences with terms ostensibly designating such things is evidence in favor of their existence, but property realism, as I have characterized it, does not itself decide these matters one way or the other.

Arguments analogous to Ackerman's may be given against the objectivity of the content/non-content distinction. Thus, one might say 'John believes that Mary is untrustworthy' might be taken in accordance with (7), (8) or (9)

(7) John believes (the proposition) that Mary is untrustworthy
(8) John believes Mary-is-untrustworthy-ly.
(9) The number 3 John-Mary-is-untrustworthy-believes.

My reply here is parallel to my previous reply. That Mary is untrustworthy can be believed, doubted, true or false, but neither John, Mary, the number 3, nor *being such that John-Mary-is-untrustworthy-believes* can have these features. And if there are things eligible for belief, *etc.*, then surely that Mary is untrustworthy is one of them. Nonetheless, content realism leaves open, for example, the question of whether there is a thing such as *that stealing is wrong*.

V. Properties And Concepts? Propositions And States of Affairs?

I now address a different concern about my definitions of 'property' and 'content'. A property, on my definition, is eligible both for being attributed and for being exemplified. A content, on my definition, is eligible both for being believed or doubted and for truth or falsity. These definitions, therefore, recognize no gap in ontological kind, respectively, between ways things could or could not be and the ways things could be thought to be, and between what is possible or impossible and what is thinkable. When a person attributes squareness to an object, and the object is square, what the person attributes is literally the same as what the object possesses. When a person believes that snow is white, and snow is white, what the person believes is literally the same as the fact that snow is white. An objector might protest: if one person attributes *being water* to something and another attributes to the same thing *being H_2O*, what they attribute is different, but nonetheless, both attributions are true of a puddle of water in virtue its possession of a single property, *viz. being H_2O*. Again, if one person believes that Hesperus is closer to the Sun than Earth and another that Phosphorus has this feature, these distinct contents believed are made true by one and the same state of affairs, *viz.* the obtaining state of affairs with respect to Venus

---

[5] A Cartwright-inspired question arises here: Why not say that some properties are attributable while some are not? See Cartwright (1962). A similar question arises in the philosophy of perception: Why not say that in non-veridical perception we directly perceive sense-data while in veridical perception we directly perceive external objects? Again in the metaphysics of speech acts: Why not say that what is asserted in some cases is a proposition, a non-linguistic entity, while in others it is a sentence? The answer in each case, I think, is that the notion in question is unitary, and so does not relate vastly different kinds of things. External objects are very different sorts of things than sense-data; direct perception, however, is unitary. Sentences and propositions are very different sorts of things; assertion is unitary. Here, too, we may say that attributable but unexemplifiable things are different sorts of things than exemplifiable things, while attribution and exemplification and unitary.

that it is closer to the Sun than Earth. What is attributable, the claim might be, are *concepts*, whereas what is exemplifiable are *properties*; what are thinkable are *contents*, whereas what are possible or impossible are *states of affairs*.[5]

Distinguishing concepts from properties and contents from states of affairs is useful in stating a kind of materialism that respects the phenomena of intentionality and mentality in general. The materialist may recognize that the *concepts* of pain and C-fiber stimulation are distinct, while claiming that they pick out the same physical property, *viz.*, C-fiber stimulation. Here are Putnam (1975) and Smart (1959):

> It seems to me that there are at least two notions of 'property' that have become confused in our minds. There is a very old notion for which the word 'predicate' used to be employed (using 'predicate' as a term only for *expressions* and never for properties is a relatively recent mode of speech: 'Is existence a predicate?' was not a *syntactical* question) and there is the notion for which I shall use the [term] 'physical property'.

> The principle of individuation for predicates is well known: the property of being P (where 'property' is understood in the sense of 'predicate') is one and the same property as the property of being Q...just in case 'x is P' is *synonymous* (in the wide sense of 'analytically equivalent to') 'x is Q'.

> Consider, however, the situation which arises when a scientist asserts that temperature *is* mean molecular kinetic energy. On the face of it, this is a statement of identity of properties. What is being asserted is that the *physical property* of having a particular temperature is *really* (in some sense of 'really') the *same property* as the property of having a certain molecular energy...If this is right, then, since 'x has such-and-such a temperature' is not *synonymous* with 'x has bla-bla mean molecular kinetic energy'...it must be that what the physicist means by a 'physical magnitude' is something quite other than what philosophers have called a 'predicate' or a 'concept'. (Putnam 1975, pp. 305-6)

> Let me...try to state more accurately the thesis that sensations are brain-processes. It is not the thesis that, for example, "after-image" or "ache" means the same as "brain process of sort X" (where "X" is replaced by a description of a certain sort of brain process). It is that, in so far as "after-image" or "ache" is a report of a process, it is a report of a process that *happens to be* a brain process. It follows that the thesis does not claim that sensation statements can be *translated* into statements about brain processes... Sensations are nothing over and above brain processes. (Smart 1959, p.170).

Correspondingly, the materialist may say that the contents <Bill is in pain> and <Bill C-fibers are stimulated> are distinct yet true in virtue of the obtaining of the same physical state of affairs, *viz.*, the state of affairs of Bill's C-fibers being stimulated.

These distinctions are also perhaps useful in accounting for the phenomena of indexical reference in language and thought within a broadly realist framework. As Frege put it, each of us is presented to himself in a special way. When I believe that

I am hungry, I represent myself as *being me*. The content of my belief is given by the pair (*being me, being hungry*). Your belief that you are hungry seems to have this very same content. If we thought such beliefs could be true or false *simpliticer*, we would have to conclude that, necessarily, my belief is true iff yours is, which is clearly not the case. Instead we should say that my belief is true, if it is, only relative to me, and yours relative to you (Sosa, 1983). But how could a content ascribing a genuine property be true only relative to a perspective? It is preferable to say that *being me* is not a way of being but a way of being conceived. *Being water* is perhaps also an indexical concept, and if so does not contribute to the ways things are but to the ways we think of them. So, generally, in indexical reference, we employ perspective-relative concepts that may determine properties but are not themselves properties.

This "perspectivism" gives us a seemingly smooth resolution of Twin-Earth problems. Two important desiderata of an account of the Twin-Earth cases are that the account explain how Oscar and Twin-Oscar think in the same way while referring to different kinds of substance. The perspectivist may claim that, when Oscar and Twin-Oscar both say 'Water is clear', they express belief in the same content, given by (*being water, being clear*), even though Oscar refers through his belief to H_2O while Twin-Oscar refers to XYZ. Of course, reference in these cases is not reference *simpliciter*, but reference relative to a perspective. Nonetheless, with this caveat, perspectivism finds relevant sameness and difference in the beliefs of Oscar and Twin-Oscar, as is required by the desiderata.

I want to consider separately the challenges posed to my account of property (content) realism by the materialist concept/property distinction and by perspectivism. The materialist may find certain consequences of perspectivism useful in developing an adequate version of her view, but for her purposes she needs a concept/property distinction that goes beyond that provided by perspectivism. Some mental characteristics are not indexical, *e.g.*, pain, but are not counted by the materialist as genuine properties.

First, the materialist challenge. Take the case of pain and C-fiber stimulation. The materialist claims that the concepts *pain* and *C-fiber stimulation* are true of a state of mind because they pick out a genuine property of it, *viz.* C-fiber stimulation. So the materialist must distinguish two entities corresponding to the term 'C-fiber stimulation', the concept and the property. This raises a worry about multiplication of entities *non gratia*. Compare the concept and the property. Both apply to objects, both have "components," if either do, the concept having as a component the concept *stimulation*, the property having the property *stimulation*. Although we cannot attribute the property, we can attribute the concept. Why should this be? Wouldn't we do better to claim that there is simply one property here, that what is attributed to a state in attributing *C-fiber stimulation* is one and the same as what is possessed by it? Perhaps the response will be that by invoking concepts in addition to properties, we allow for a distinction between concepts that present properties as they are in themselves and those that do not. But how does the concept *C-fiber stimulation* present *C-fiber stimulation* as it is? What accounts for this? It might be claimed this is accounted for by the fact that the components of the concept and property correlate one-to-one under the relation of *reference*. Now consider a "simple"physical concept, one which lacks components. It seems at least logically possible for there to coexist a distinct concept, perhaps mental, which itself is simple but which does not refer to the relevant physical property. But what could explain the fact that one refers while the other does not? Appeal to causal/nomological relations does not seem to help. For it could be that tokenings of both concepts could be related in the right way to tokenings of the property. Moreover, it is not even necessary to invoke simple concepts and properties. As long as there is an isomorphism between a pair of concepts, one that presents the property as it is and one that does not, and an isomorphism between each concept and the property, the problem remains. For, presumably, the physical concept presents the property as it is because its fundamental components present the fundamental components of the property as they are. Yet it is unclear what would disqualify the fundamental components of the other concept from presenting those of the property in their true light.

Further confirmation that concepts would be *entia non gratia* is obtained by observing materialist uses of the concept/property distinction. The distinction is invoked by Kim (1996) in a discussion of the problem of mental causation. For Kim, mental "features,"if viewed as concepts rather than properties, can be explanatorily relevant without being causally relevant. Any explanation of a piece of behavior by reference to the instantiation of a mental property M will be true in virtue of the causal relevance of M's realizer, not of M itself, since it is not a property. I ask: How can the following symmetry be broken?

> *Taking M to be a higher-order property, we say*: M is not a causally potent property. Its same-level realizer P seems to do all the work. Thus, 'M caused the behavior' is literally false. Nonetheless, 'M explained the behavior' may be true, if we allow that a property A can *explain* a property B (with respect to a causal interaction) by virtue of having a realizer that causes B.

> *Taking M to be a higher-order concept that is not a property, we say*: M is not causally potent, since no concept is causally potent. Thus, 'M caused the behavior' is literally false. Nonetheless, 'M explained the behavior' may be true, if we allow that a concept A can *explain* a property B (with respect to a causal interaction) by virtue of having a realizer that causes B.

The same theoretical work that can be done with the concept/property distinction can be accomplished with a division among properties of the causally impotent and the causally potent. But if this is so, and the concept/property distinction introduces additional metaphysical difficulties, why not stay with the distinction among properties?

One motivation for moving to the concept/property distinction is the need to find an adequate description of reductions in science. If we do not accept the division of concepts and properties, how are we to explain the scientist's statement that temperature is mean molecular kinetic energy? As Putnam (1975, p. 306) points out in the passage previously quoted, this looks like a statement of identity of properties, and yet what is expressed by the predicate '*x* has such-and-such a temperature' is not the same thing as what is expressed by 'x has bla-bla mean molecular kinetic energy'. Putnam concludes that we need two notions of "property," the notion of what is expressed by a predicate (a concept) and the notion of what is a real feature of objects (a genuine property).

Putnam's crucial move is to apply either the schematic principle

Being F = Being G iff 'is F' and 'is G' are synonymous

or its relatives

F-ness = G-ness iff 'is F' and 'is G' are synonymous
F-ing = G-ing iff 'F' and 'G' are synonymous

to the case of temperature and mean kinetic energy. One may either question the principle or its application. The two views I will discuss both question its application.

Non-controversially, the schematic letters 'F' and 'G' can be instantiated only to predicate expressions. But neither expressions of the form 'temperature T' nor those of the form 'temperature T' are predicate expressions. Expressions of the form 'Has temperature T' are, however. Still, as is suggested in Tye (1981), one cannot use the principle to which Putnam appeals to justify the transition from the premise that the expressions 'has temperature T' and 'has mean kinetic energy E' are non-synonymous to the conclusion that temperature T is not mean kinetic energy E. The only conclusion one may reach is that *having temperature T* is not the same as *having mean kinetic energy E*.

So Putnam's argument fails. Yet still one wonders how temperature T could *be* mean kinetic energy E, since it seems one could attribute having a temperature of 100 degrees Celsius without knowing much of anything about what mean kinetic energy is. So there remains a problem of explaining how there could be an identity here. I will discuss two plausible explanations, one descriptivist and the other Kripkean.

The descriptivist thinks as follows. We may see the singular terms of the form 'Temperature T' as short for indexicalized definite descriptions of the form 'the property that is F', where 'F' includes an indexical term such as 'here' or 'us', as in 'measured by reading R of such-and-such of our instruments'. Thus, the open sentence 'x has temperature T' is analytically equivalent to something of the form 'x has the property that is F'.

Following Tye (1981), the descriptivist might think of the indexical element as 'in our world', and so say that a scientist's statement

(10) Temperature T = mean molecular kinetic energy E

is best parsed as something of the form

(11) The property *in the actual world* that fulfills such-and-such role = mean molecular kinetic energy E

where '*E*' is a rigid and non-descriptive designator. However the index is conceived, the descriptivist may retain the identity condition for properties in terms of synonymy (or, better, attribution) *and at the same time* say that (10) states an identity of properties. For it is of a type with 'The Empire State Building is the tallest building in our state', or 'The virtue most rarely instantiated around here is courage'. Although the property *being the virtue most rarely instantiated around here* is distinct from the property *courage*, courage is identical with the virtue most rarely instantiated around here.

Yet this sort of response will not enable us to understand the scientist's *general* statement 'Temperature is mean kinetic energy' as an identity statement. The descriptivist, however, may say that temperature is a determinable whose determinates are the various temperatures. Thus, it seems, '*x* has temperature' will mean the same as '*x* has some temperature property'. If the various expressions 'temperature *T*' are then understood as equivalent to expressions of the form 'the *F*-property', with '*F*' containing an indexical, '*x* has temperature' must be understood as equivalent to something of the form '*x* has some *G*-property', where '*G*' draws out what is common to the various *F*-properties of the various temperatures, thus retaining their indexical element. Given all this, one *might* think the general statement 'Temperature is mean molecular kinetic energy' would have to be interpreted as equivalent to 'The property of having some *G*-property is the property of having some mean molecular kinetic energy'. The latter is false, given the synonymy criterion. Suppose, for example, that '*G*' is 'measured by our thermometers'. The predicates '*x* has some property measured by our thermometers' and '*x* has some mean molecular kinetic energy' would not be synonymous according to the descriptivist, and this for a reason that does not concern the details of our replacement of '*G*': the properties expressed are different insofar as one who attributes *having some property measured by our thermometers*—say before the discovery of molecules—may not even grasp the property *having some mean molecular kinetic energy*, and so will be able to attribute it to anything. And even if one grasps both properties, one might wrongly believe that the air surrounding him has some property measured by our thermometers but that the same air does not some have mean molecular kinetic energy, say because one believes that air is a vacuum.

Consider an analogy. Suppose there is a seven-paged book, which we have dubbed 'B', that lists the seven deadly sins, the name of each being given on a separate page. Suppose that sloth is named on page 3. Then, of course, to attribute sloth would be to attribute the property that is in fact named on page 3 of B. However, the statement 'Having sloth is having the property in fact named on page 3 of B' is false. Someone acquainted with book B, but mistaken about the page on which 'sloth' appears, might well believe 'pride' is written on page 3 and so attribute *having the property in fact named on page 3 of B* to someone but, noting the proud person's industriousness, deny *having sloth* of him. In the same way, one could attribute *having temperature T* to something while denying *having mean molecular kinetic energy E* of it. Dwelling further on B, we may note that, for each of the seven deadly sins, there is some number n such that the sin is *the property in fact named on page n of book B*. But *having one of the seven deadly sins* would still not be identical to *having a property in fact named on some page of book B*. In the same way, one could attribute *temperature* to something without attributing *mean molecular kinetic* energy to it.

So if one individuates properties in terms of synonymy, and one accepts strong Fregean conditions on synonymy, one cannot accept the received view that the scientist's statement

(12) Temperature is mean molecular kinetic energy

states the identity of temperature and mean molecular kinetic energy. But one need not, for that reason, deny that (12) is an identity statement. One may say instead that the statement is best construed as stating that *each temperature is identical to some mean molecular kinetic energy*. One thereby sees the scientist as stating a *general* identity proposition—a proposition of the form *that every F is identical to a G*—rather than a *particular* one—one of the form *that a is identical to b*.

Admittedly, descriptivism faces problems. As is clear, the sample description given in terms of the readings of our instruments will not cut the temperatures finely enough. A better thought, perhaps, is that only certain temperatures are picked out through descriptive material relating to the observable, *e.g.*, the temperatures at which water boils and freezes. Other temperatures are picked out in relation to these temperatures. This thought is best developed using the method of Ramsification. One introduces all the temperatures at once but connects only a few "by definition" to the observable. Certain difficulties will need to be faced: how to spell out the connections with the observable—*e.g.*, are they direct or indirect?, can the view capture the cardinality of the set of temperatures?; how can we answer the question, 'Whose thinking about temperatures does this capture—that of the average American adult, of the student of thermodynamics?' Considering these difficulties, one might be tempted to abandon hope. But in defense of descriptivism, it is scarcely easy to shake off the familiar Fregean intuition that statements of the form 'Temperature T = mean kinetic energy E' state profoundly interesting, and certainly non-trivial, pieces of information.

Kripkeanism sees expressions of the form 'temperature T' as *de jure* rigid designators, but ones whose references are fixed by, but not synonymous with, certain definite descriptions.[6] Kripkeanism can be more precisely formulated by invoking the apparatus of two-dimensional modal semantics. Applied to the sentence '100 degrees Celsius will not boil alcohol', Kripkeanism delivers not merely one intension, which involves a rigid description, as the descriptivist would have it, but two intensions, a primary one involving the unrigidified description associated with the sense of '100 degrees Celsius' and a secondary one involving the property *designated* by '100 degree Celsius'. On the level of primary intensions, reduction statements of the form 'Temperature T = mean kinetic energy E' would state descriptive facts. On the level of secondary intensions, though, they would state non-descriptive identity facts.[7] To

---

[6] For Kripke's Kripkeanism, see Kripke (1980), Lecture III.

[7] For an illuminating treatment of the primary/secondary intension distinction as it bears on theoretical reduction, see Chalmers (1996).

grasp the meaning of an expression 'temperature T' one needs only to know its primary intension. So, the skeptic of or predecessor to the molecular theory of gases and the rest of modern chemistry could have thought without irrationality that 100 degrees Celsius is not mean kinetic energy so-and-so, even though in fact it is and necessarily so.

But the details of Kripkeanism are less important than the following general, if somewhat vague, point. The Kripkean thinks of expressions like '100 degrees Celsius' as functioning in a fashion similar to proper names. At least initially, and in many cases beyond that time, a name fixes on an object in virtue of the fact that the object satisfies a certain definite description—perhaps even one that competent users of the name must grasp—and yet the name is not synonymous with the description. Thus, if 'temperature T' and 'mean kinetic energy E' are name-like, just as one can believe without irrationality that Mark Twain is not Samuel Clemens, even though Twain is Clemens, so one can believe without irrationality that temperature T is not mean kinetic energy E, even though T is E. This is not to say that there is no difficulty here for the Kripkean. But if the analogy with names holds good, solving the Fregean problems facing Kripkeanism about proper names will likely enable the solution of the Fregean problems facing Kripkeanism about natural kind terms such as our 'temperature T'.

We now turn to the perspectivist. Note that here it would not be especially damaging to admit the existence of perspectival "concepts." These might just be reckoned as of a kind with other properties, yet distinguished as properties that apply only relative to perspectives. A perspectivist need not distinguish the attributable from the exemplifiable: she might simply emphasize that the class of properties—of attributable, exemplifiable things—includes some things that are exemplifiable only relative to a perspective.

However, if there remains a nagging suspicion that perspectival "properties"would not be genuine constituents of the world, another response to the perspectivist is available. This is to account for indexical reference without appeal to perspectival notions. I have no such developed account. I can only point out the advantages of a Russellian approach that invokes Russellian propositions as the contents of indexical beliefs. Here is a first attempt at such a theory:

> (13) S believes that he himself is F iff S believes the Russellian proposition given by the pair (S, F-ness).

It might be asked what S believes if he has a demonstrative belief the demonstratum of which is himself, e.g., if S believes *he* is a shabby fellow, to use a familiar example, not realizing that he himself is the demonstratum of the demonstrative [he[, say because he is unwittingly seeing himself in a mirror. One who accepts (13) cannot supply the same Russellian proposition as the content of S's demonstrative belief that *he* is F. These beliefs have different impacts on action and participate in different inferences. In the example, S's belief that *he* is a shabby fellow would have little impact on S's feelings about himself, unlike a belief on the part of S that he himself is a shabby fellow. One solution is to say that the demonstrative *he*, as used in S's thought, does not refer directly, but through certain descriptive elements. We might say that, as used by S, *he* is identical with the property *being the person I am now seeing*. This property itself is Russellian, since it contains as a constituent both S himself and the present time.

Alternatively, we might assign the same Russellian proposition as content to the thought by S that he himself is a shabby fellow and his thought that *he* is a shabby fellow, but revise our original Russellian account of indexical reference. What follows, however, is less an account or explanation of indexical reference than a set of directions for identifying the phenomenon. (14) tells us the ways indexical reference is not achieved, but leaves open the question of the way(s) in which it is achieved:

> (14) S believes that he himself is F iff, S has a belief B such that (i) the content of B is the Russellian proposition given by the pair (S, F-ness), and (ii), B is about S but not in virtue of S's being related to himself by any relation of mental attention nor in virtue of S's possession of empirical information about himself the causal source of which is himself.

(14) enables us to distinguish indexical reference in thought from demonstrative reference, descriptive reference, and reference through a proper name. I can grasp a Russellian proposition about the apple before me only because I possess empirical information that both stems from the apple and is about it. The empirical information I have about myself plays no part in explaining how I can grasp in indexical self-reference a Russellian proposition about me. I can grasp a Russellian proposition about an after-image of red, a "red after-image," only because I am mentally attending to it.

The above thoughts are promising, I think, but remain on the level of the speculative. If they cannot be satisfactorily developed, we would perhaps be justified in conceding to the perspectivist that *being me* and the rest apply only relative to a perspective. Still, one need not divide the attributable and the exemplifiable: we might say that indexical properties, if there are such things, are like other properties in being both attributable and exemplifiable, but differ in that they are exemplifiable only relative to a perspective.

CHAPTER 2

Deflationism Rejected, Weak Deflationism Presented

In the first chapter, I gave a partial defense of realism about properties and propositions. In this chapter and the next, I make use of the apparatus provided by such realism to propose an account of truth. The account I will propose, Weak Deflationism, draws from both correspondence and deflationist theories. It "deflates" truth for propositions, the basic truth-bearers, but "inflates" truth for entities that express propositions. Central throughout the chapter will be the views of Paul Horwich (1990). Weak Deflationism attempts to incorporate a basically Horwichian deflationism about truth for propositions within the framework of a correspondence theory of truth for other kinds of truth-bearers.

My plan for this chapter is as follows. I will first examine deflationism and present it in what seems to me its most plausible form. I will then argue that deflationism, so understood, is an inadequate theory of truth, because it lacks the resources to explain facts deriving from the dependence of truth upon meaning. This will be followed by a description of Weak Deflationism.

Truth, say the deflationists, is not deep or substantial, and so no traditional philosophical analysis should be sought for it. How is truth to be explained, then? One common deflationist line runs as follows. The meaning of 'true' is fully explained by an account of its function, which is to serve as a device for abbreviating infinite conjunctions and disjunctions. Here is Michael Williams:

> [W]hen we have pointed to certain formal features of the truth-predicate (notably its 'disquotational' feature) and explained why it is useful to have a predicate like this (*e.g.*, as a device for asserting infinite conjunctions), we have said just about everything there is to be said about truth. (Williams 1988, p. 424)

This view, which we will call 'disquotationalism', seems to be endorsed in these well-known passages from Quine:

> By calling the sentence ['Snow is white'] true, we call snow white. The truth predicate is a device of disquotation. We may affirm the single sentence by just uttering it, unaided by quotation or by the truth-predicate; but if we want to affirm some infinite lot of sentences that we can demarcate only by talking about the sentences, then the truth predicate has its use. We need it to restore the effect of objective reference when for the sake of some generalization we have resorted to semantic ascent. (Quine 1986, p. 12)
>
> Ascription of truth just cancels quotation marks. Truth is disquotation. (Quine 1992, p. 80)

Disquotationalists maintain in support of their view that if indeed truth-predicates were devices for abbreviating infinite conjunctions and disjunctions, the utility of truth-generalizations would be readily explainable as follows. When we wish to affirm a sentence that we can identify only indirectly, or an infinite lot of sentences, we can use generalizations of the form 'The F is true' or 'Every F is true' as abbreviations of the corresponding infinite conjunctions of the forms "If 'Snow is white' is the F, then snow is white & if 'Water is wet' is the F, then water is wet &..." and "If 'Snow is white' is an F, then snow is white & if 'Water is wet' is an F, then water is wet &...". By asserting such infinite conjunctions we make conditional commitments to the sentences we wish to assert; so, *e.g.*, by asserting 'The first sentence Fran uttered is true', I express a commitment; keeping to it requires me to accept the first sentence Fran uttered if I learn its identity.

The deflationist, however, need not accept disquotationalism, for she need not accept one of its corollaries, *i.e.*, that truth-predicates in various languages do not express the same property, and so do not express a property, *truth*.[1] She may instead allow that truth-predicates express the property of truth but insist on deflating this property. Her project will be to explain truth itself by reference to such simple

---

[1] If truth-predicates are devices for abbreviating infinite conjunctions and disjunctions, then if 'true' and 'vrai' express properties, they express different properties, 'true' expressing the disjunctive property of *being either identical to 'Snow is white' and such that snow is white or identical to 'Snow is red' and such that snow is red or...*and 'vrai' expressing the property of *being either identical to 'La neige est blanche' and such that snow is white or identical to 'La neige est rouge' and such that snow is red or...*

There is a place, on the disquotationalist view, for talk of a "property of truth." 'Truth' might be stipulated to denote the property that truth-predicates have in common, *i.e.*, the property of having such-and-such abbreviatory function. Note, however, that 'truth', so used, would denote a property of truth-predicates, not a property *expressed* by truth-predicates.

A note about my use of the word 'property'. I use 'property' to denote the sorts of entities that are expressed by predicates (exemplifiables, attributables). I do not presuppose that properties are "universals," repeatable entities that are fully present where exemplified. Nor do I wish to rule out the view that Michael Devitt and Georges Rey call 'selective realism,' according to which we can raise metaphysical questions about whether wrongness, for example, is a property in some metaphysically loaded sense. (See Devitt and Rey 1991, p. 95.) I use 'property' inclusively to pick out both "natural" and "unnatural" properties. However, I realize that using 'property' to denote entities at all brings some metaphysics with it.

schemata as *'p' is true iff p* and *It is true that p iff p*.[2] These schemata cannot be transformed into closed sentences expressing candidate analyses or elucidations (where a candidate elucidation of a property *F*-ness, let us say, purports to exhibit constitutive non-analytic connections between properties, *i.e.*, connections expressible by sentences of the form *For all x, x is F...ϕx*' where what replaces '...' is either 'if', 'only if' or 'iff'[3]).[4]

There are advantages to this *property* deflationism. Consider what is involved in taking true to be a mere device of abbreviation. Claims of abbreviation entail claims of meaning equivalence, and as Gupta has argued, truth-generalizations such as 'Everything Sarah said is true' and their corresponding infinite conjunctions, 'If Sarah said that snow is white, then snow is white & if...', are not equivalent in meaning.[5] The property deflationist, by contrast, recognizes that such generalizations express genuinely universal propositions, and explains the utility of truth-generalizations in expressing conditional commitments by appealing to the simple equivalence schemata.[6] Property deflationism has a further advantage: it has no need to justify withholding from truth-predicates the title of *expressing a property*. I will be concerned with this more liberal, more attractive brand of deflationism. In what follows, 'deflationism' will refer exclusively to property deflationism.

The guiding thought underlying deflationism is that truth in its various applications is to be explained by reference to the appropriate equivalence schemata, for example:

Truth for Sentences	*'p' is true iff p*
Truth for Propositions	*<p> is true iff p*[7]
Truth for Beliefs	*A belief that p is true iff p*
Truth for Utterances	*An utterance of 'p' is true iff p*

---

[2] I use italics to mention schemata. The schematic letter *'p'* should be understood here and throughout as accepting as fillings declarative sentences of English which are not vague, ambiguous, or context-dependent. We will be investigating deflationary accounts of truth for the most unproblematic truth-apt declarative sentences.

[3] Hilary Putnam's "informal elucidation" of truth in terms of justification under ideal epistemic circumstances is a biconditional version (See Putnam 1981, p. 55).

[4] More generally, we might say that to deflate a property is to explain it by reference to simple schemata that cannot be transformed into closed sentences expressing analyses or elucidations. Thus, a deflationist about meaning might attempt to explain meaning by reference to the schema *'p' expresses the proposition that p*.

[5] They are not conceptually equivalent: one could understand the truth-generalization and not understand the infinite conjunction. (See Gupta 1993.) Nor are they even logically equivalent.

[6] The property deflationist emphasizes the following argument schemata in accounting for the utility of truth-generalizations

Everything *X* uttered is true	What *X* uttered is true
X uttered *'p'*	*X* uttered *'p'*
'p' is true	*'p'* is true
∴ *p*	∴ *p*

[7] I follow Horwich in treating the schema *<p> is true iff* p and *It is true that p iff p* as conceptually equivalent. One might wish to qualify this, however, since some philosophers will

Let us ask, then, what it would be to so explain truth.

At the very least, the deflationist aims to provide a *recipe* for explaining, for specified truth-bearers, what it would be for them to be true: a sentence (proposition, *etc.*) is specified, and then the relevant instance of the relevant schema is asserted. The recipe for sentences would be this: for any suitable (English) sentence S, specify S by its quote name, then assert the instance of the disquotation schema containing that quote name.

A recipe for explaining, however, is not a theory. A theory of truth is a proposition or totality of propositions involving truth that purports to *be* an explanation of truth. It is not too much to require that philosophers attempting to give objective accounts of truth formulate, or at least identify, theories of truth. For, plausibly, to explain truth is to provide a theory that is an explanation of truth.[8] But how can the deflationist formulate or identify a theory? The schemata 'p', <p>, *the belief that p, an utterance of* 'p' are dummies for *English* expressions, but there are truth-bearers that are not denoted by any English expression. Similarly, the schema p accepts as instances only English sentences, while there are propositions that are not expressed by English sentences but which serve as truth-conditions for truth-bearers. For these reasons alone, and independently of the problem of circularity, it does no good to try to formulate deflationist theories by the use of substitutional quantification, *e.g.*, as in "For all p, 'p' is true iff p", or for propositions, 'For all p, <p> is true iff p'.

If the deflationist is to identify a theory, she must appeal either to possible extensions of English or to propositional forms. The appeal to possible extensions of English is viciously circular. To make clear how these extensions solve the problem of truth-bearers whose truth-conditions cannot be specified in present English, for example, one would have to insist that the extensions of English contain sentences that express these truth-conditions. The deflationist does better to turn to propositional forms.

Following Horwich, I shall say that propositional forms or "structures"are functions from entities to propositions and are expressed by schematic sentences (Horwich, 1990, p. 19). Thus we have

Schematic Sentence	*Propositional Form*
"'p' *is true iff p*"	<'p' is true iff p>
'<p> *is true iff p*'	<<p> is true iff p>
'*A belief that p is true iff p*'	<A belief that p is true iff p>
"*An utterance of* 'p' *is true iff p*"	<An utterance of 'p' is true iff p>

We then state what it is to be a proposition of a certain form in terms of being a value of the form for some argument(s). Thus, <p&q> is a function, CONJ, which, given

---

reject <p> *is true* while accepting *it is true that p*, because they doubt there is such a thing as the proposition that p. To be safe, we might work with the schema If <p> *exists, it is true iff p*. I will ignore this complication in what follows. On the connections between 'it is true that p' and 'that p is true', see Kent Wilson's discussion of "extraposition"(Wilson 1990, section II).

[8] I add the qualification "objective"to emphasize that we are concerned only with philosophers whose aim is to give an account of the *property* of truth.

propositions *P* and *Q*, returns a proposition CONJ(*P*, *Q*). A proposition is of this form iff it is the value of CONJ for a pair of arguments. Horwich apparently conceives such forms as basic constituents of propositions, which contain positions that may be filled in either by Fregean senses or by the referents of such senses (concrete objects, properties, propositions, *etc.*). But whether or not we have reason to conceive of such forms as literal constituents of propositions, we ought to recognize structure among forms. Some forms "decompose" into others. Thus, for example, the form <(*p* & *q*) v *r*> decomposes into CONJ and DISJ. Accordingly, we may think of the form <<*p*>is true iff *p*> as the function, E-prop, which is decomposable into the functions IFF and Tr in such a way that for all propositions *P*, E-prop(*P*) = IFF(Tr(*P*), *P*). IFF is construed in a manner parallel to CONJ and DISJ, and Tr is to be the propositional function that takes an entity and returns the proposition with respect to it that it is true. The values of Tr thus are propositions attributing truth to an entity directly, not through the mediation of a "sense."[9] We then take a proposition to be of the form <<*p*> is true> just in case it is the value of Tr for some proposition as argument; for example, <<Snow is white> is true> is the value of Tr for <Snow is white>. Consequently, E-prop(<Snow is white>) = <<Snow is white> is true iff snow is white>.

Analogously, the equivalence form for sentences, <'*p*' is true iff *p*>, E-sent, decomposes into the functions IFF, Tr, and EXP. EXP takes an entity as argument and returns the proposition it expresses.[10] For any suitable sentence *S*, E-sent(*S*) = IFF(Tr(*S*), EXP(*S*)). E-sent ('Snow is white') = <'Snow is white' is true iff snow is white>.[11]

---

[9] If one wished to avoid commitment to Russellian (*de re*) propositions, one might try to recast Tr as a function from entities to propositions that attribute truth to individual concepts, or perhaps essences, that pick out their objects in *propria persona*. For a theory of propositions that allows for direct aboutness while repudiating the idea that propositions are complex in any sense, Bealer (1998). According to Bealer, a Platonist theory allows that the singular predication to an object of being self-identical, for example, yields a "seamless" proposition that is directly about the object but which does not contain it as a constituent; such a proposition would exist even if the object it is in fact about does not.

[10] To be precise, we would need to bring in a reference to natural languages here. We would say that EXP is a two-place function taking sentences and languages and returning the proposition expressed by the sentence in the language. Thus, following Lewis (1975), I distinguish between natural and abstract languages. A natural language is a datable, conventional activity wherein words are used to mean. An abstract language is a triple of a domain of signs, of meanings, and a function from signs to meanings. Thus, under deflationism about sentential truth, what it is for a sentence S of a natural language NL to be true is given by the value of the interpretation function corresponding to the abstract language L determined by NL. So, for 'Snow is white', the deflationist has it that what it is for it to be true is given by the proposition that snow is white. I will avoid these complications of natural and abstract languages throughout the chapter.

[11] The equivalence forms for beliefs and utterances are not as easily characterized. But the following might point in the right direction. We work with functions UG, IF*, BEL, and IFF*, where these are partly characterizable as follows:

There is work to be done in clarifying the notion of a propositional form. But we can already put our rough machinery to work on behalf of the deflationist. She may now identify her theory by reference to propositional forms. She may say, following Horwich, that her theory of truth for propositions consists of all and only the propositions of the form <<p> is true iff p>,[12] that her theory of truth for sentences consists of all and only the propositions of the form <'p' is true iff p>, *etc.* These theories are infinite and cannot be formulated.

Nonetheless, the deflationist *need* not follow Horwich here. Ernest Sosa proposes a finite, minimal theory, (FMT), that quantifies over propositions (Sosa 1993, pp. 177-95).[13]

UG is a function taking properties into propositions: UG(being round if red) = <Whatever is red is round>). IF* is a function that takes pairs of properties into properties: IF*(being red, being round) is the property of being round if red. BEL is a function taking propositions into properties: BEL(<Snow is white>) = the property of being a belief that snow is white. IFF* is a function from pairs of properties and propositions into properties: IFF*(being red, <Snow is white>) = the property of being red iff snow is white. Given all this, we may say:

E-belief(P) = UG(IF*(BEL(P), IFF*(Truth for beliefs, P)))

(An example: the value of E-belief for <Snow is white> is the proposition that everything is such that if it is a belief that snow is white then it is true iff snow is white).

E-utt(S) = UG(IF*(Utt(S), IFF*(Truth for utterances, EXP(S)))

(An example: the value of E-utt for 'Snow is white' is the proposition that everything is such that if it is an utterance of 'Snow is white' then it is true iff snow is white).

[12] A qualification concerning the liar-like pathologies is needed. Perhaps we should follow Horwich in stipulating that no proposition that would generate paradox is an axiom of the theory. (See Horwich 1990, pp. 41n2.) However, whether a proposition would generate paradox or not is in some cases a contingent matter, so there is no a priori method for identifying all and only the problematic propositions. For more on the liar-like pathologies, see Chapter 6. In what follows, this qualification is to be understood as implicit.

[13] In a recent paper, Donald Davidson (1996, p. 273) writes:

> Why, though, does Horwich not try generalizing his schema by quantifying over propositions? The answer should be: because then we would have to view ordinary sentences as singular terms *referring* to propositions, not as *expressing* propositions.

But why should this be? In general, one who accepts propositions as values of objectual variables of quantification, need not regard them as the referents of sentences. Perhaps Davidson's claim is that there is no way to generalize Horwich's schema without using sentential variables, so that the only eligible generalization would be 'For all p, <p> is true iff p'. If this is his claim, it is falsified by (FMT). Davidson then turns to what he calls the "crux":

> How are we to understand phrases like 'the proposition that Socrates is wise'? In giving a standard account of the semantics of the sentence 'Socrates is wise', we make use of what the name 'Socrates' names, and of the entities of which the predicate 'is wise' is true. But how can we use these semantic features of the sentence 'Socrates is wise' to yield the reference of 'the proposition that Socrates is wise'? (1996, pp. 273-4)

(FMT) For all propositions P, P is necessarily equivalent to the proposition that it is true.

To derive instances of the schema <p> *is true iff* p, Sosa invokes a principle of entailment, (PE):

(PE) If <p> entails <q>, then if p, then q. (1993, pp. 187-8)[14]

Although Sosa is non-committal on these matters, it appears the deflationist does best to construe (PE) as a principle of inference rather than as a disguised substitutional quantification or as shorthand for an infinite list of principles. Read as a disguised substitutional quantification, (PE) is no longer an unproblematic resource, since it records a fact about truth, one that presumably needs explanation. Read as shorthand for an infinite list, generality is compromised. Furthermore, (PE) should be read as applying, to both Russellian and Fregean proposition-designators. Thus, it licenses inference from 'The proposition that Hesperus is a planet entails the proposition that there is a planet' to 'If Hesperus is a planet, then there is a planet' regardless of whether 'the proposition that Hesperus is a planet' is read as *the proposition, with respect to Hesperus, that it is a planet.*

The deflationist cannot use precise analogues of (FMT) for truth for sentences and utterances, however, for several reasons, the most obvious of which is that there is no workable analogue for sentences or utterances of the notion of "the proposition, with respect to x, that it is true." We cannot speak intelligibly of "the sentence, with respect to x, that it is true." The best that can be done is to speak of a sentence of an extension of English consisting of a name for x concatenated with 'is true'. However, given our function Tr, and assuming a relation of material implication not explained in terms of truth—an assumption Horwich makes[15]—we may employ a relative of Sosa's theory that avoids such problems. Consider the finite theory, (FT):

FT-Sent	For all sentences S, EXP(S) is materially equivalent to Tr(S)
FT-Prop	For all propositions P, P is materially equivalent to Tr(P)
FT-Belief	For all beliefs B, if B is a belief in P, then P is materially equivalent to Tr(B)
FT-Utt	For all utterances u, if u is an utterance of S, then EXP(S) is materially equivalent to Tr(u)[16] [17]

These are difficult questions, and to answer them adequately, one would need to provide a semantic theory grounded in a theory of propositions. For our purposes, though, it may be enough to say this: for any unproblematic declarative sentence of English, S, the singular term resulting from the application the operator 'the proposition that...' to S *refers* to the entity which is *expressed* by S. Thus, there are features of the semantics of 'Socrates is wise' that can be used to yield the reference of 'the proposition that Socrates is wise'.

[14] Horwich employs a principle analogous to (PE), but for material implication Horwich (1990, p. 23).

[15] Horwich (1990, p. 23).

[16] In FT-Sent and FT-Utt, and throughout the remainder of the essay, I let the qualification "suitable" go implicit.

[17] Perhaps the theory (FT) could be simplified further, as follows:

To derive instances of the various equivalence schemata, we may employ a principle of material implication, (PMI):

(PMI)   If <p> materially implies <q>, then, if p, then q

Other unproblematic premises will be needed in these derivations, among which will be sentences such as "<Snow is white> = EXP('Snow is white')"and "Tr('Snow is white') =<'Snow is white' is true>."

So by invoking propositional forms, deflationists can identify and even formulate theories of truth. These theories will yield purported explanations of truth for particular truth-bearers. Thus, for any proposition P, a deflationist theory of truth for propositions, whether finite or infinite, will yield the proposition E-prop(P), which cites the proposition P as *explanans* of Tr(P). If E-prop(P) is formulatable, the deflationist may assert it. But formulatable or not, the deflationist maintains that E-prop(P) is an explanation of what it is for P to be true; she defends this by saying that what E-prop(P) cites as explanans of Tr(P) is the explanans of P.

Two comments on this use of 'explanation'. First, the term here does not have its usual factive implication with respect to the *explanandum*. In asserting that <'Whales are fish' is true iff whales are fish> is an explanation of <'Whales are fish' is true>, the deflationist is not implying that 'Whales are fish' is true. What are purportedly explained are *propositions* attributing truth, which themselves may or may not be true. A similar use of 'explanation' is useful in discussion of analyses. It is natural to say that analyses are explanations, so that an analysis <To be F is to be G> cites G-ness as *explanans* of F-ness. But an analysis does not entail that the *analysandum* is exemplified; an analysis <To be F is to be G> does not entail that F-ness is exemplified. Moreover, an analysis of F-ness may be said to have as consequences propositions that are explanations of what it is for particular entities to be F. Thus, if knowledge is analyzed in terms of justified true belief, then <Gary knows that whales are fish iff Gary believes truly and with justification that whales are fish> is an explanation of <Gary knows that whales are fish>. It identifies as *explanans* <Gary believes truly and with justification that whales are fish>.[18] On behalf of the deflationist, we use 'explanation' to ascribe an analogous a priori, philosophical explana-

---

For all propositions P, P is materially equivalent to Tr(P)
For all truth-bearers x, if x is not a proposition, then EXP(x) is materially equivalent to Tr(x)

A possible disadvantage of this theory, in contrast to FT, is that it may hide the structure of truth for non-propositional entities. So, for example, perhaps truth for utterances is explainable in terms of truth for sentences.

[18] Ernest Sosa has suggested to me that this use of 'explains' as relating propositions, regardless of their truth-value, would connect with ordinary usage better if it were regarded as abbreviatory of 'would explain'. Thus, for example: Gary's knowing that whales are fish would be explained by his believing truly and with justification that whales are fish.

There seem to be good reasons to acknowledge non-philosophical, *a posteriori* relations of explanation between propositions, *e.g.*, the relation between what is expressed by the conjunction of the premises of a Hempelian Deductive-Nomological explanation and what is expressed by its conclusion.

tion relation holding between propositions such as <Snow is white> and <'Snow is white' is true>.

Second, and relatedly, we assume that the explanation relation picked out by our use of 'explanation' implies material equivalence. Thus, if <Whales are fish> is explained by <'Whales are fish' is true>, the two are materially equivalent. So it is with analyses. If *F*-ness is analyzed (and so explained) by *G*-ness, then whatever is *F* is *G* and vice versa..

Lest it be objected that, because the values of <'*p*' is true iff *p*> and the other equivalence forms are symmetric with respect to the "right-"and "left-hand"propositions, they fail to cite either proposition as *explanans* of the other, we should note that the deflationist may choose instead take the following asymmetric forms as foci for her theories:

Truth for Sentences	<<*p*> explains Tr('*p*')>[19]
Truth for Propositions	<<*p*> explains Tr(<*p*>)>
Truth for Beliefs	<For any belief *B* in <*p*>, <*p*> explains Tr(*B*)>
Truth for Utterances	<For any utterance *u* of '*p*', <*p*> explains Tr(*u*)>

An asymmetric finite theory, (AFT), is then formulatable:

AFT-Sent	For all sentences S, EXP(S) explains Tr(S)
AFT-Prop	For all propositions P, P explains Tr(P)
AFT-Belief	For all beliefs B, if B is a belief in P, then P explains Tr(B)
AFT-Utt	For all utterances u, if u is an utterance of S, then EXP(S) explains Tr(u)[20]

To derive instances of the various equivalence schemata, one would invoke the principle:

For all X, if <*p*> explains Tr(X), then X is such that it is true iff *p*

Using this principle, for example, one may derive "'Whales are fish' is true iff whales are fish"from "<Whales are fish> explains <'Whales are fish' is true>."

So we see that the deflationist attempts to explain truth as applied to truth-bearers of each kind by identifying a propositional form which is such that, for each truth-bearer of that kind, there is a proposition of that form which is an explanation of the proposition that it is true. This strategy is common to finitistic and infinitistic deflationists.

If *this* is the sort of explanation of truth the deflationist aims to provide, we must ask whether it would be all the explanation we may legitimately demand from

---

[19] The form <<*p*> explains Tr('*p*')>> can be thought of as the function F from sentences to propositions such that F(S) is the ordered pair, ((EXP(S), Tr(S)), explaining). The form for propositions can be construed similarly *mutatis mutandis*. I shall not attempt construals of the forms cited above for beliefs and utterances.

[20] Again, perhaps (AFT) admits of a simplification:

For all propositions P, P explains Tr(P)
For all truth-bearers, x, other than propositions, EXP(x) explains Tr(x)

There is a disadvantage here analogous to that discussed in note 17.

a theory of truth. We need a standard for judging whether a deflationist explanation of a property would be explanation enough. Here is Paul Horwich on this point:

> The primary test of [minimalism] (and any other) theory is its capacity to accommodate the phenomena in its domain. That is to say, if our theory is a good one, it will be able to account for all the facts about truth. (1990, p. 22)

Horwich gives us a necessary condition: a theory of truth, deflationist or otherwise, provides explanation enough only if all the facts about truth (that need explaining[21]) can be explained on its basis. The theorist of truth may use other unproblematic theories and facts in this enterprise, *e.g.*, facts and principles of logic, of epistemology, *etc.* The task is to show that one's theory, in conjunction with unproblematic theories and facts, entails in a sufficiently simple and comprehensive way all the facts in need of explanation.

Note that an *analysis* of a property would automatically meet this necessary condition. For, equipped with an analysis, a theorist may simply substitute *analysans* for *analysandum* in fact-expressing sentences (or at least in all such sentences that do not involve hyperintensional contexts), and the resulting sentence will express an *explanans* of the fact expressed by the original sentence. Thus, suppose knowledge is analyzed by justified true belief. Then facts about knowledge of the form <Knowledge is *F*> that need explanation are explained by corresponding facts of the form <Justified True Belief is *F*>. Facts predicatively involving knowledge of the form <...knows...> are explained by the corresponding fact of the form <...believes truly and with justification...>. As we will see in § 3, matters are not so simple for the deflationist, especially for the infinitistic deflationist. Deflationist theories no doubt address the particular facts involving truth—the facts that are values of Tr—but it is not clear *that* or *how* they address general facts involving truth.

Deflationism is attractive. It is simple and economical. It makes possible swift and obvious derivations of instances of the various equivalence schemata. It seems to hit the mark in characterizing truth as simple, devoid of any deep metaphysical or empirical nature. And if it should prove tenable, we would perhaps better understand why, historically, there has been such disagreement over how to analyze truth.

Deflationism in this generalized form, however, is problematic. Troubles arise with vague, ambiguous, context-sensitive, and non-factual declarative sentences (if there are any), as well as with the liar-like pathologies. But its most serious problem is its inability to explain facts deriving from the dependence of truth on meaning. The problem is nothing new, but its importance seems not to have been sufficiently

---

[21] This qualification is necessary for several reasons. First, there are facts involving truth that seem to need no explanation. Suppose knowledge is analyzable as justified true belief. Then the fact that, for all propositions *P*, someone knows *P* iff he has justified true belief in *P* seems not to stand in need of explanation. It is, as I will say, a "fact of analysis." What does need to be explained, and to be explained by a theory of truth, is how truth contributes to the nature of knowledge, *i.e.*, how the involvement of truth in knowledge underwrites facts such as the fact that if Gary knows that whales are fish, then whales are fish.

appreciated by deflationists.[22] And it can be appreciated simply by examining obvious facts about the English language.

English sentences, like all sentences, have the truth-conditions they do *because* they mean what they do, and they mean what they do as a matter of convention. This conventionality, moreover, insures that any sentence might have had a meaning that determined truth-conditions different from (and perhaps even incompatible with) the truth-conditions determined by the sentence's actual meaning. For example, 'Snow is white' might have meant that grass is red, and so have been true iff grass were red. Conventionality of meaning thus engenders contingency of *truth-conditions*. Because the propositions expressed by instances of the disquotation schema give the truth-conditions for sentences, they too come out contingent. So if one attempts to account for the facts involving truth for sentences solely by reference to the form <'p' is true iff p> (or for that matter, the form <<p> explains Tr('p')>) and other unproblematic resources, then certain important facts will go unaccounted for—including all facts expressed by instances of the schema *Possibly, not-('p' is true iff p)*. Here the deflationist's unproblematic resources might be allowed to include propositions of the form <'p' expresses <p>>. The most important limitation on such resources, of course, is that they not contain an analysis or elucidation of truth for sentences in terms of a substantial notion of meaning, where a substantial notion of meaning is a notion of meaning that is not explainable by reference to a deflationary schema such as 'p' expresses <p>. But this is just what is needed. *Contra* Quine, truth is more than disquotation.[23] *Contra* the deflationists, truth for sentences needs to be analyzed or elucidated in terms of substantial meaning.

This inadequacy of deflationism does not spring from an inability to *generalize* explanations of particular facts to yield explanations of general facts. Deflationism cannot even account for particular facts such as the fact that 'Snow is white' might not have been true iff snow is white, let alone the general fact that the values of E-sent are contingent. Contrary to deflationism, the values of E-sent are not explana-

---

[22] The problem is in the background of the discussions of T-sentences by Etchemendy (1988, pp. 60-1), and Soames (1995, pp. 252-3).

[23] A similar conclusion can be reached for our grasp of truth. Our grasp of truth is not exhausted by our disposition to readily accept with justification instances of the disquotational schema. We also readily accept with justification instances of the schema *Possibly, not-('p' is true iff p)*. This acceptance cannot be explained or justified simply by appeal to our justified acceptance of instances of the disquotational schema.

Note that the existence of these modal facts also seems to count against Hartry Field's (1994a) claim that sentences of the form "'p' is true"are cognitively equivalent to the corresponding sentences of the form 'p'. The sentences "'Snow is white' is true"and 'Snow is white' are not cognitively equivalent in a strong sense, which involves their being inter-derivable *tout court*, for they are not so inter-derivable. The derivation of one from the other requires a further assumption about meaning. That assumption may be common knowledge, but it is necessary all the same if the derivation is to be valid. If in speaking of "cognitive equivalence,"Field has in mind a more liberal relation, which permits the use of auxiliary "common knowledge"assumptions in derivations of one from the other, then Field's claim is non-controversial, but not deflationist.

tions of propositions attributing truth to English sentences. <Snow is white> does not explain <'Snow is white' is true>, and in general, there is no English sentence S such that EXP(S) explains Tr(S).[24]

It may be helpful here to consider how these considerations tell against some views expressed in a recent essay by Horwich (1995). Horwich makes little mention (if any) of meaning in his accounts of sentential truth, *being true of* (i.e., predicate satisfaction) and reference. About the latter two concepts, Horwich writes:

> ...virtually no matter what is substituted for "F" or "N", it is uncontroversial that
>
> "F" is true of something iff it is F
>
> and
>
> "N" refers to something iff it is identical to N
>
> According to the deflationary point of view there is nothing more to our concepts of *being true of* and *reference* than is conveyed by our acceptance of these schemata. (1995, p. 359)

But let us consider the dependence relations between such concepts and that of meaning. Take the case of *being true of*. A predicate has the extension it does because it has the meaning it does. *That* a predicate means what it does, moreover, is a matter of convention, and so contingent fact: a predicate may in fact mean F-ness but have possibly meant G-ness, rather than F-ness, where these properties are distinct, perhaps incompatible. This appears to make good sense on Horwich's preferred "use" theory of meaning: any predicate might have been used in relevantly different ways and so have meant something very different from, and perhaps incompatible with, what it in fact means.[25] This feature of meaning insures that the instances of the schema

'F' if true of something iff it is F

---

[24] Recall that we are using 'explains' to express a kind of *a priori*, philosophical explanation relation that holds between propositions independently of whether they are true, and which bears an analogy with the relation between an *analysans* and an *analysandum*.

Perhaps it is unsurprising that <Snow is white> fails to explain <'Snow is white' is true> in the required *a priori* fashion. The former, after all, does not entail the latter. This shows that (AFT) is false and not merely explanatorily inadequate.

[25] Horwich does accept a version of the doctrine that meaning determines extension, namely this: no difference in extension without a difference in meaning. What needs to be added to derive the contingency of the propositions expressed by instances of the schema 'F' *is true of something iff it is F* is the assumption that any predicate could have meant some property that was not exemplified by all and only the things that exemplified the property the predicate actually means. This assumption can be seen to be acceptable if we focus on the possibility that any predicate could have meant a property that was a contrary to the property it in fact means, *e.g.*, 'Red' could have expressed being-green. Horwich does not discuss this assumption. However, it seems a mere artifact of the fact of the conventional character of the meaning of linguistic items.

express contingent facts. So for example, 'red' might have not been true of something iff it were red, but, say, iff it were blue; 'cat' might not have been true of something iff it were a cat, but, say, iff it were a bird. Although these seem to be just the consequences we want, intuitively, they are not welcome to a deflationist like Horwich. They point to the failure of accounts that attempt to explain *being true of* by reference to the propositional form corresponding to the deflationary schema above (using only unproblematic resources). Important facts involving *being true of*, deriving from its dependence on meaning, are left unaccounted for. Horwich is right to emphasize the "uncontroversial" or obvious nature of the propositions expressed by instances of this schema, and of the propositions expressed by instances of the corresponding schemata for reference and truth,[26] but obviousness does not insure explanatory adequacy.

Two distinct objections might be raised at this point. The first asks why such modal facts need to be explained at all. If a theory of truth needs to explain all the facts *that need explaining*, some reason must be given for thinking that the modal facts in question need explaining, if the criticism of deflationism is to stick. The second objection grants that the modal facts need explaining, but asks why they cannot be explained by means of a simple addition to the deflationist account of all the relevant modal propositions (if the theory is infinite) or of some appropriate modal universal proposition (if the theory is finite).[27]

In reply to the first objection, we may say that the relation between truth and meaning is an obvious, a priori, substantial dependence relation. A theory of truth should have something to say about it. There is something about truth and its relation to meaning by virtue of which the relevant modal propositions come out as a priori and obvious facts. Refusal to explain these modal facts deriving from truth's

---

[26] Horwich is not altogether satisfied with the use of the disquotation schema here. In a footnote he writes:

> More accurately, one ought to speak of a sentence as *expressing a truth* rather than as *being true*; and it is in this first sense that I intend my use of the truth-predicate to be understood. (1994, p. 358n]

To talk of *expressing a truth* would seem to build in a reference to meaning. But even when the disquotation schema is replaced by a schema framed in terms of this notion, the dependence of truth on meaning is unacknowledged. Horwich's preferred schema would seem to be (1):

(1) '*p*' expresses a truth iff *p*

But instances of this schema will express contingent propositions. What is needed to accommodate the dependence of truth on meaning is a schema

(2) '*p*' is true iff '*p*' expresses a truth

(2) is readily transformed into a traditional analysis of truth for sentences in terms of meaning and truth for propositions.

[27] The infinitistic deflationist could not accommodate all of the relevant modal facts merely by adding all of the propositions of the form <Possibly, not-('*p*' is true iff *p*)> to her account. Nor would it be enough for the finitistic deflationist to add the proposition <For no sentence

constitutive link to meaning is analogous to refusal to explain, in one's account of causation, facts deriving from the constitutive link to laws.

The second objection presents an intriguing possibility. The relevant modal propositions are obvious and *a priori*. What is then to stop one from incorporating them into the deflationist account? The problem is that elements of the resulting theory would be in tension. One element of the theory would assert a material equivalence, and another would assert or imply the contingency of that material equivalence. The tension would consist in the fact that the theory prompts, but offers no answer to, the question, '*Why* is there material but not necessary equivalence?'

Hartry Field (1994b) offers a third sort of response to the "contingency" objection. He proposes that the deflationist take counterfactuals such as

(1) If we had used 'Snow is white' in certain very different ways, it would have had the truth conditions that grass is red.

to have as their "cash value" statements such as

(1-CV) In considering counterfactual circumstances under which we used 'Snow is white' in certain very different ways, it is reasonable to translate it in such a way that its disquotational truth conditions relative to the translation are that grass is red. (1994b, p. 277)

Field's strategy is thus to conceive of the relevant modal intuitions as special cases of intuitions about truth in other languages. We are to treat the language used by our counterfactual selves—in the relevant world—as another language, truth in which can be explained in the same way as truth in actual other languages.

How does (1-CV) help the deflationist answer the contingency objection? Field claims that (1-CV) captures the content of (1), so that by affirming (1-CV), the deflationist affirms the contingency intuitions. But the issue is not simply whether the deflationist can affirm the intuitions, but whether she can *explain* the facts these intuitions register. Field says nothing about how the deflationist might account for (1-CV). In substituting (1-CV) for (1), therefore, Field substitutes one *datum* in need of explanation with another no less in need of explanation. We need to be told *why* it is reasonable to translate 'Snow is white' as used under such counterfactual circumstances in the way (1-CV) outlines. Field offers no guidance on this crucial matter. The obvious explanation of (1-CV) would be that in suitable counterfactual situations, 'Snow is white' is used by us to *mean* that grass is red. Of course, that explanation is unavailable to Field. How else can (1-CV) be explained? Presumably, we

---

S is EXP(S) necessarily equivalent to Tr(S)>. These propositions do not entail any facts of the form <Possibly, 'p' is true and not-p> or of the form <Possibly, 'p' is not true and p>. Some, but not all, of the latter propositions are facts, *e.g.*, <Possibly, 'Snow is white' is true and snow is not white> is a fact, but <Possibly, '7 + 5 = 12' is true and 7+5≠12> is not. So the deflationist cannot simply make her additions based directly on the forms <Possibly, p is true and not-p> or <Possibly, p is not true and p>. The relevant form will be this, it seems: <(If, possibly, not-p, then, possibly, 'p' is true and not-p) & (if, possibly, p, then, possibly, 'p' is not true and p)>. Instances of this form, in conjunction with unproblematic modal facts, will entail the relevant modal facts involving truth.

are to look to pragmatic "rules of translation."This seems to falsify the objective character of intuitions such as the intuition that 'Snow is white' might have been true iff grass is red. But no matter, there is a more serious problem in the offing.

We might have been able to conceive properties which we cannot in fact conceive, and so we might have used some of the predicates we actually use to pick out such properties; for example, we might have been capable of experiencing a finer discrimination of colors, in which case we might have used 'is white' to ascribe a color property that is not expressed by any of our predicates. If this is possible, then 'Snow is white' might have been false and untranslatable by any sentence in our language, even though snow was white. Our rules of translation would be of no help to us. Yet we have an unmistakable conviction on this matter, deriving from our convictions about the relation between truth and meaning.

The Fieldian deflationist cannot avoid the above problem even by appealing to a notion of objective synonymy. Such an appeal would involve the proposal of the following explanation schema for explaining facts such as that recorded by (1):

(i) There are counterfactual situations in which 'p' as used by us (there) has the same meaning as 'q' as actually used by us.
(ii) If 'p' as used by us in a counterfactual situation has the same meaning as 'q' as actually used by us, then in that counterfactual situation 'p' as used by us (there) is true iff q
(iii) There are counterfactual situations in which 'p' as used by us is true iff q.

The instances of this schema have the virtue of avoiding the seemingly irrelevant issue of "reasonableness of translation." Still these instances, collectively, are not adequate to explain all the relevant modal facts that need explaining. Some of these facts outrun the facts about objective synonymy relations between sentences as used by us in counterfactual situations and sentences as actually used by us.

Generalized or *strong* deflationism, then, is unable to explain certain important facts deriving from the dependence of truth on meaning. But while this inability beleaguers generalized deflationism, it does not afflict deflationism restricted to truth for propositions. If one is willing to inflate meaning, one can give an account of truth for non-propositional entities that recognizes explicitly a dependence on meaning, but which remains deflationist about truth for propositions. Truth for non-propositional entities will be analyzed in terms of the expression of true propositions. This is Weak Deflationism.

How precisely the deflationist component of Weak Deflationism should be identified is a difficult and somewhat peripheral question. There are several options. One could affirm either Horwich's infinite theory, Sosa's finite theory (FMT) (*i.e.*, the theory that for all propositions P, P is necessarily equivalent to $Tr(P)$), the finite theory (FT), which is similar to Sosa's except that it employs the notion of material equivalence, or the finite theory that every proposition of the form $<<p>$ is true iff $p>$ is necessary.[28] Alternatively, one could take as the focus for one's theory the asymmetric form $<<p>$ explains $<<p>$ is true$>$. One might then affirm the theory

---

[28] This option is unavailable to the strong deflationist in her theory of truth for sentences, since propositions of the form $<'p'$ is true iff $p>$ are contingent.

(AFT) (*i.e.*, the theory that for all propositions P, P explains Tr(P)) or the theory that every proposition of the form <<p> explains <<p> is true> is necessary. I leave unanswered the question of which of these theories is best. Weak Deflationism is thus a determinable theory of truth.

Weak Deflationism is deflationist about key *ontological* notions. To deflate propositional truth is to deflate facthood; to deflate *being true of* (as a relation between properties and individuals) is to deflate exemplification.[29] Propositional truth and *being true of* are two of a kind, and Weak Deflationism deflates them both. This is not to rule out the possibility of substantive ontological debate, only debate about facthood or exemplification. Under Weak Deflationism, these cannot serve as cornerstones of ontology.

The account I am proposing is similar to the "primitivist"theory of truth, defended at times by Moore and Russell, according to which truth is a simple, unanalyzable property. On both views, propositional truth is deflated and non-propositional truth is inflated.[30] The primary point of difference lies in Weak Deflationism's ability to take account of facts of the form <<p> is true iff p>. Accounting for these facts helps to answer questions that bothered Russell: Why should we seek to believe propositions that have this simple property of truth? Why is possession of this simple property valuable? Russell complains of his "primitivist"theory that

> [it] *seems* to leave our preference for truth a mere unaccountable prejudice, and in no way to answer to the feeling of truth and falsehood.[31]

If truth is what Weak Deflationism says it is, then it is no wonder why we seek to believe propositions that have this simple property. An example will suffice. Those of us who live near the coastline wish to believe that a hurricane is in the forecast when a hurricane is in the forecast; and if we believe that a hurricane is in the forecast when <A hurricane is in the forecast> is *true*, we will believe, as desired, that a hurricane is in the forecast when a hurricane is in the forecast.

A final word on Horwich's views. Horwich apparently accepts a substantial notion of meaning as use, but does not put it to work in explaining the dependence of non-propositional truth on meaning (1995, p. 356). But if one employs a substantial notion of meaning, then why not hope for analyses or elucidations of non-propositional truth? Is this not part of the very *raison d'être* for employing a substantial notion of meaning? Horwich seems to think that to put a notion of meaning to such a use is to violate one of the fundamental insights of the deflationist approach to truth:

> Minimalism involves the contention that truth has a certain purity—that our understanding of it is independent of other ideas. (1990, p. 12)

This purity, as we have seen, is a feature only of propositional truth.

---

[29] Horwich (1994, p. 74) also gives a deflationary schema for exemplification.
[30] I rely on the account of the Moore-Russell view given by R. Cartwright (1987a, p. 73). Sosa (1993) defends the Moore-Russell view.
[31] This passage is quoted by Cartwright (1987a, p. 73).

CHAPTER 3

Questions for Weak Deflationism

Questions (1)—(7) are some of the principal questions that *need* to be answered by a Weak Deflationist:

(1) Is Weak Deflationism circular?

(2) Why shouldn't one seek a correspondence theory of propositional truth?

(3) Does Weak Deflationism stumble on the explanation of *general* facts involving truth?

(4) Does Weak Deflationism have the resources to explain the obviousness of the propositions expressed by instances of the schema '*p*' *is true iff p*?

(5) Can the Weak Deflationist answer the standard objection to correspondence theories that if truth consisted in correspondence with the facts, knowing is true would require an absurd comparison between sentences (utterances, beliefs) and facts?

(6) Is Weak Deflationism incompatible with non-factualist theories of certain areas of declarative discourse, *e.g.*, moral discourse?

(7) Why can't we use higher-order quantification to formulate deflationism about truth as a universalized biconditional?

I reserve discussion of three larger topics for later chapters: (i), Can we analyze propositional truth in terms of concrete worlds?; (ii), Doesn't the demand for truth-makers for true propositions jeopardize deflationism about propositional truth?; and (iii), How can Weak Deflationism cope with the liar-like pathologies?

I. Is Weak Deflationism Circular?

Weak Deflationism is a version of the traditional correspondence theory, distinguished (perhaps) by its deflationism about propositional truth. Correspondence theories have often taken one of the following forms. (Here, for simplicity, we restrict our attention to sentences, and in particular, to atomic sentences).

(A) An atomic sentence is true iff it represents (means) a state of affairs that obtains.

(B) An atomic sentence is true iff it attributes to a n-tuple of objects $(x_1,..., x_n)$ an n-ary relation R, and R holds of $(x_1,..., x_n)$.

The charge of circularity is based on the claim that the talk of states of affairs "obtaining" in (A) and of relations "holding of" n-tuples in (B) is disguised talk of truth and being true of. Now the correspondence theorist, whether she is a Weak Deflationist or not, should accept the grounds just given for the charge of circularity, but reject the charge itself. She should admit that talk of states of affairs "obtaining"and relations "holding of" n-tuples is disguised talk of truth and *being true of*, and so accept the objector's rewriting of her theory. However, she should rebut the charge of circularity by saying that the notion deployed in explaining sentential truth—whether it is "obtaining" or "exemplification" or propositional truth—is not sentential truth itself but a more basic truth-like notion.[1] The same goes for Weak Deflationist explanations of non-propositional truth.[2]

It might be thought the Weak Deflationist account of propositional truth fails to be explanatory insofar as its formulation makes use of notions (entailment or material implication) that must themselves be understood in terms of truth. Adam

---

[1] One might think that correspondence theories of the same sort as (B) would not need to invoke any notion of truth in the *analysans* of truth for sentences. Following this line, one might replace (B) with (B*):

(B*) A sentence is true iff it attributes an n-ary relation R to a ordered n-tuple of objects $(x_1,...,x_n)$ and $R(x_1,...,x_n)$.

(B*), however, is not well-formed, 'R' occurs first as a singular term and then as a predicate. To achieve the desired analysis, one would need to replace (B*) with (B**)

(B**) A sentence is true iff it attributes an n-ary relation R to a ordered n-tuple of objects $(x_1,...,x_n)$ and $(x_1,...,x_n)$ exemplifies R.

This is not an improvement. In (B**), the talk of "exemplifies"serves the same function that talk of "holding of"serves in (B).

[2] Clarity, at times, may require us to signal this distinction in writing. We might use 'TRUE' to express propositional truth, 'TRUE' to express non-propositional truth, and 'true' to denote the disjunction of these. Thus, we would say: to be true is to be TRUE or TRUE, and to be TRUE is to express a TRUE proposition. I do not mean to imply that non-propositional truth itself is unitary. Perhaps good arguments can be given to show that truth for utterances, for example, depends on truth for sentences, which in turn depends on truth for beliefs. There may be an interesting structure to non-propositional truth.

Kovach (1997) raised this objection to Weak Deflationism in his paper "Deflationism and the Derivation Game." One of my principal aims in "Weak Deflationism" was to show that given Horwich's resources, the deflationist can do what Horwich said she cannot: she can *formulate* deflationism. Horwich allows himself the resources of material implication relations between propositions and a notion of broadly logical necessity that is not understood in terms of truth.[3] Yet all would be for naught, if Horwich's resources were not legitimately available to the deflationist. So let us consider, separately, the cases of entailment and material implication.

Kovach mentions that entailment, as a relation between propositions, is typically explained in terms of truth. How would such an explanation run? What we need is a notion of broad logical entailment, not entailment by virtue of logical form. But it appears that, barring the invocation of *possibilia*,[4] our attempted explanations leave us with a residual necessity. We say: For all P, Q, P entails Q iff, *necessarily*, if P is true, Q is true. Nor does there seem to be a way to explain *necessity* in terms of truth, without adverting to entailment. So we must work either with a truth-independent notion of necessity or a truth-independent notion of entailment. But given either of these, we may define the other without appealing to truth, by means of one of the following principles:

For all P, Q, P entails Q iff IF(P,Q) is necessary.

For all P, P is necessary iff, for all Q, Q entails P.

(There is an advantage to taking entailment as the basic notion. One can use it, together with other truth-free materials, to characterize the logical forms CONJ, NEG, DISJ, IF, and so on. Taking necessity as basic incurs the debt of explaining IF without invoking entailment. This is a point I neglected to mention in my response to Kovach (1997).) The deflationist's appeal to entailment, then, seems legitimate. The same goes for appeals to *making probable* and *bringing about* as relations between propositions (facts). In both cases, residual notions of probability and causality appear in attempted analyses.

Kovach's doubts about material implication are better founded. Material implication and truth are interdefinable, at least in the sense under which a definition provides a necessarily equivalent condition. (We may define material implication thus: For all P, P materially implies Q iff, if P is true, then Q is true. See Kovach's (TMI) for a definition of truth in terms of material implication.) Of course, such definitions

---

[3] For the use of a relation of material implication, see Horwich (1990, p. 23). For remarks about the explanatory independence of necessity from truth, see Horwich (1990, pp. 22-23).
[4] I do not present a criticism of Lewis-style modal realism here. I only say that if Lewis's modal realism were true, and if propositions were sets of *possibilia*, propositional truth would be analyzable, contrary to deflationism:
For all propositions P, worlds W, P is true at W iff W is a member of P
In Chapter 4, I argue against this proposed analysis of truth and its concomitant notion of proposition.

may fail to qualify as philosophical analyses. But their availability raises questions about the explanatory independence of material implication and truth.

So suppose the deflationist were denied appeal to material implication in formulating her theory and giving explanations. What would be lost? Deflationism is better formulated in terms of entailment or explanation relations, in any case. Moreover, it seems that the principle of entailment, (PE), can be used to do much, if not all, the essential work done by (PMI) in giving explanations of facts about truth. This will become clear, I hope, in the sections of this chapter to follow.

II. Why Shouldn't One Seek a Correspondence Theory of Propositional Truth?

Suppose one claimed that propositions, independently of their truth-value, represent states of affairs, and that their truth and falsity consists in the "obtaining" or not of the corresponding states of affairs. How would one then explain what is it for a state of affairs to obtain? If this notion, too, is given a correspondence analysis, we have started down an infinite regress of substantial truth-like notions.

The correspondence theorist might wish to deny that the truth of a proposition depends on a representation relation to a entity which holds whether or not the proposition is true. Thus, one hears talk of "facts," "events," "property-instances," as distinguished from true propositions. Where propositions are held to be abstract, and so in some sense not really "in the world," events are held to be concrete worldly entities that are perceivable and form the causal nexus. A correspondence theorist might insist that truth finds its basis in precisely such worldly entities. He might offer the following analysis of propositional truth:

(C) For any proposition P, P is true iff P corresponds to an event.

I think this is a dead end for several reasons. First, there are problems with negation. If one allows that <Snow is white> is true in virtue of a relation to an event, e, then it seems one must also allow that <Snow is not white> must be true in virtue of a relation to a distinct fact, e', where e and e' *exclude* one another. What would explain the exclusion? It seems that the explanation must run along these lines: e and e' have a common content, which obtains in the case of e and does not obtain in the case of e'; talk of "e"and "e'," that is to say, is indistinguishable in meaning from talk of truth and falsity of one and the same proposition.

Perhaps the correspondence theorist has a response. He may insist that a plausible correspondence theory of propositional truth will have to deny that there are events corresponding to true negative propositions. (C) will give way to a recursive theory that explains truth for atomic propositions in terms of correspondence to events, and truth for molecular propositions in terms of the truth of their constituent propositions, *etc.*

Second, and more seriously, the (C)-theorist cannot derive from his analysis instances of the schema for propositional truth. Some deflationist theory of propositional truth must be strictly added, prompting the question, 'why do we need the analysis if we have the deflationist theory?' Correspondence relations are vitally important in explaining the dependence of non-propositional truth on meaning. Propositions, however, do not have meanings; they *are* meanings.

Third, it is not clear what such a relation of correspondence would be. The correspondent for a basic proposition <Socrates is white>, it seems, would have to be something like *Socrates's whiteness*. Thus there would be the following necessary connection: necessarily, if *Socrates's whiteness* exists, then <Socrates is white> is true. Correspondence between propositions and events would be merely supervenient.

Mystery about such correspondence is avoided if the schematic (C*) is substituted for (C):

(C*) Atomic proposition <*a* is *F*> is true iff the event of *a*'s being *F* exists

(I ignore the complications of time.) But, as we have seen, the correspondence theorist must also add a deflationist theory in order to derive instances of the schema:

(E-atom) Atomic proposition <*a* is *F*> is true iff *a* is *F*

From the correspondence theory based on (C*) and the added deflationist theory, then, one may derive any instance of

(E-event) The event of *a*'s being *F* exists iff *a* is *F*

This seems to get things backwards. The instances of (E-event) are not mere consequences of a theory of truth; they purport to give explanations of atomic facts in terms of facts about the existence of events. Consequently, it seems that (E-event), together with (E-atom), purports to explain (C*).

The thought emerging here is that events do not enter into the explanation of propositional truth by virtue of being correspondents of true propositions, but enter, if at all, into the ontological explanation of atomic truths themselves. When an ontologist asks what makes a proposition true, he is not concerned with any correspondence relation, nor it seems even with truth; he sees that an object is red, round, *etc.*, and wants to know what entities there are such that their *existence* explains the object's redness, roundness, *etc.*[5] More exactly, he wants to know something highly schematic. Allowing that his schema may be filled in by sentences expressing true atomic propositions, he supposes that *a* is *F*, asks "Why is *a* F?", and seeks an answer that identifies, schematically, the entities whose existence explains the fact that *a* is *F*? Yes, *a* must exist, and so must *F*-ness; these must be combined in some way; there must be an event of *a*'s being *F*. Here truth serves only to *identify* what needs explaining. The ontologist is not concerned, at least in the first and most basic instance, to explain truths about what is true, but rather to explain truths themselves.

---

[5] This view of the "truthmaker"ontologist is similar to that expressed by Fox (1987). Fox proposes the following "truthmaker"principle on p. 189:

If *p*, some x exists such that x's existing necessitates that *p*

I would only add that the ontologist seeks entities whose existing *explains*, and not only necessitates, the relevant truth.

See Chapter 5 for a more extensive discussion of the truthmaker project in ontology.

We have found no good reason for an ontologist or anyone else to accept a correspondence theory of propositional truth. But let me note, finally, that *were* we to find otherwise, we would still find ourselves forced to accept a view akin to Weak Deflationism. Suppose we maintained that what it is for a proposition to be true is for it to correspond to an event. Thus, <*a* is *F*> is true iff it corresponds to an event of *a*'s being *F*. To derive the conclusion that *a* is *F* from the premise that <*a* is *F*> is true, we would need our principle (E-event). But now what do we say about event existence? If we think of existentials about events as analyzing atomic predications, then the resulting view is still Weak Deflationist, for all we would be doing is reconstruing propositions as asserting the existence of events. But if we are not to claim an analysis here—if we are to resist returning to Weak Deflationism—we must take account of the event equivalences of the form (E-event). The only way to do this is to affirm a deflationist theory about event existence. Thus, where E is a function from atomic predications to their corresponding event existentials, we would have:

> For all atomic *P*, *P* is necessarily equivalent to the proposition with respect to *P* that the value of E for *P* as argument exists.

The moral is that one must be a deflationist with respect to the fundamental truth-like property. If truth for propositions is the fundamental such property, then it must be deflated; if we must look to existence for events, then it must be deflated.

III. DOES WEAK DEFLATIONISM STUMBLE ON THE EXPLANATION OF GENERAL FACTS INVOLVING TRUTH?

Let us begin by considering the various types of general facts involving truth that might be considered in need of explanation.

(G1) General facts relating truth to its modalities, *e.g.*, the fact that if a proposition is true, then it is possibly true.

(G2) General facts relating truth to falsity, *e.g.*, the fact that if a proposition is true it is not false.

(G3) General facts concerning what can and cannot bear truth, *e.g.*, the fact that only propositions can be true.[6]

(G4) General facts relating truth to the semantic and the psychological, *e.g.*, the fact that all true beliefs are beliefs in true propositions, the fact that what is known is true, the fact that the propositions expressed by instances of the disquotation schema are obvious.

(G5) General facts concerning truth and logic, *e.g.*, the closure of truth under entailment, the fact that for any propositions P, Q, CONJ (P, Q), is true iff P and Q are true, the fact that every proposition of the form <Everything is F or not-F> is true.

---

[6] The need to explain facts involving ineligibility for truth is stressed by Gupta (1993a, p. 364)

Weak Deflationism yields explanations of (G1) facts, when conjoined with theories of the modalities *simpliciter* and definitions of the truth modalities of truth in terms of amodal truth. Thus, *e.g.*, the general fact that every true proposition is possibly true may be explained by taking possible truth to be defined in terms of amodal truth as follows:

Proposition P is possibly true $=df$ Possibly, P is true

Using the biconditional obtainable from this definition, in conjunction with the modal fact that

For all P, if P is true, then possibly, P is true

the Weak Deflationist may infer that

For all P, if P is true, then P is possibly true.

The modal fact invoked in this explanation does not itself require explanation by reference to the theory of propositional truth. It derives from the general modal fact that actuality implies possibility.[7]

(G2) facts can perhaps be explained by appeal to an analysis of falsity according to which to be false is to be a proposition that is not true. (See Horwich 1990, p. 74)[8]

(G3) general facts do pose a problem for Weak Deflationism as it stands, but a minor one. The finitistic Weak Deflationist may add a condition ruling out non-propositional entities from being candidates for propositional truth. For the sake of clarity, let us use 'TRUE' in this paragraph to express propositional truth and 'TR' to denote the function that takes an entity and returns the proposition that it is true. Thus, 'For all P, P explains TR(P)' may be replaced with 'For all x, if x is a proposition, then x explains TR(x), and if x is not a proposition, then x cannot be TRUE'. The infinitistic Weak Deflationist may add to her theory the proposition that only propositions can be TRUE. Modified appropriately, Weak Deflationism yields explanations of (G3) facts and their instances, *e.g.*, the fact that no horse is TRUE, as well the fact that the moon is not TRUE. Given analyses of non-propositional truth in terms of TRUTH, explanations are available for facts such as the fact that no horse is true.[9]

---

[7] The theory of propositional truth *will* need to be invoked to explain the fact that if <Snow is white> is true, then possibly, snow is white, and other such facts. But these explanations are forthcoming: because <<Snow is white> is true> is necessarily equivalent to <Snow is white>, <Possibly, <Snow is white> is true> entails <Possibly, snow is white>; and so <If <Snow is white> is true, then possibly, <Snow is white> is true> entails <If <Snow is white> is true, then possibly, snow is white>.

[8] This definition may turn out to be inadequate. In addressing the problems of vagueness, for example, the Weak Deflationist may wish to admit propositions that are neither true nor false. She might then have to simply admit the primacy of the general facts <For all P, if P is true, then P is not false> and <For all P, if P is false, then P is not true>. To avoid contradiction, classical logic would have to be abandoned. This would be a heavy price to pay. Field (1994a) discusses some alternative deflationist treatments of vagueness that are consistent with classical logic.

[9] This answers a query by Gupta (1993a, pp. 363-4).

(G4) facts, for the most part, can be explained by reference to the Weak Deflationist's theory of non-propositional truth, and/or her independent theories of the human mind and language, possibly together with general logical facts involving truth. Thus, for example, the fact that all true beliefs are beliefs in true propositions can be explained by reference to the fact of analysis that a belief is true iff it has its content a true proposition. The fact that what is known is true is explained by reference to a theory of knowledge which includes truth in the nature of knowledge.

Many other philosophically important (G4) facts can be explained in a similar fashion, *e.g.*, the fact that there are propositions whose truth does not depend on me, the fact that justified beliefs are likely to be true, and, as we will see in a subsequent section, the fact that the propositions expressed by instances of the disquotation schema are obvious. Some cannot, however. Consider Horwich's deflationary explanation of the general fact

(Success)   True beliefs about how to attain our goals tend to facilitate success in achieving them.

Horwich considers a particular example involving a person, Bill. Horwich asks us to suppose that Bill nods because he wants a beer and believes he will get one if he nods. If Bill's belief is true, Bill will get a beer if he nods. So since he nods, he gets what he wants, a beer. Horwich then adds

And this sort of explanation may be universalized to show in general how true beliefs engender successful action. (1990, p. 24).

Gupta (1993b, p. 66) protests that Horwich offers only "an explanation of the instances of (Success), not of (Success) itself." The best Horwich's theory can offer are explanations for each of the instances of (Success). Generalizations are not logically equivalent to conjunctions of their instances, and so to explain a conjunction of all of the instances of (Success) is not to explain (Success) (Gupta 1993b, p. 63). Similar concerns can be raised concerning any general fact that needs explanation but cannot be explained simply by appealing to unproblematic principles and/or facts of analysis and elucidation. These, let us say, are the *problematic general facts*. Among them are (G5) facts as well as some (G4) facts, *e.g.*, (Closure).

(Closure)   For all propositions, P, Q, P entails Q and P is true, only if Q is true.

Gupta's reasoning would lead to the conclusion that Horwich can only supply explanations for instances of (Closure), not of (Closure) itself.

If Gupta is right, it would seem to follow that infinitistic Weak Deflationism would stumble over the explanation of any and every problematic general fact. Such facts, however, would in principle present no essential difficulty for finitistic Weak Deflationism. Let me explain.

The best the *infinitistic* Weak Deflationist can offer by way of an explanation of a problematic general fact is an explanation form, expressed by an explanation schema. Consider (Closure). Using the following unproblematic principles:

(PMI) If <p> entails <q>, then if p, then q

the infinitistic Weak Deflationism can provide the explanation schema (ES):

(ES)
(1) CONJ(<p>, <q>) entails <p> Fact of logic

(2) Tr(CONJ(<p>, <q>)) entails Tr(<p>) Wk. Defl.

(3) <CONJ(<p>, <q>) is true> entails <<p> is true> Nec. eq. of (3)

(4) If CONJ(<p>, <q>) is true, then <p> is true (4), (PE)

Because of the infinitary character of (1)—(4) under infinitistic Weak Deflationism, (ES) cannot be transformed into an argument whose conclusion is a universally quantified sentence expressing (Closure).

Finitistic Weak Deflationism, on the other hand, allows for such a transformation. I illustrate with (ES).[10] I use 'x' and 'y' are objectual variables in the following universal proof.

(1) CONJ(x,y) entails x Fact of logic

(2) Tr(CONJ(x,y)) entails Tr(x) Wk. Defl.

(3) <CONJ(x,y) is true> entails <x is true> Nec. eq. of (2)[11]

(4) If CONJ(x,y) is true, then x is true (3), (PE)

(5) For all x, y, if CONJ(x,y) is true, then x is true (4), Univ. Pf.

A similar explanation can be formulated for (Success).[12] Finitistic Weak Deflationism thus seems not to be subject to Gupta's critique.[13]

---

[10] In what follows, for ease of reference, we allow ourselves to use '<P is F>', where 'P' is a variable, as short for 'the Russellian proposition with respect to P that it is F'. Thus, where 'P' and 'Q' are variables, we will use '<P is true>' in place of 'Tr(P)' and '<P materially implies Q>' in place of 'the Russellian proposition with respect to P, Q, that P materially implies Q'.

[11] Since 'x' and 'y' are objectual variables, (3) must be given a Russellian reading, as follows: x and y are such that their conjunction entails with respect to x that it is true. Recall that (PE) may be used in connection with Russellian proposition designators.

[12] First, (Success) must be formulated more precisely. Horwich and Gupta seem to think of it as follows:

(Success) For all propositions P, Q, and individuals x, CONJ(<x believes IF(P, Q)>, <IF(P, Q) is true>, <x wants Q>, <x brings about P because x has this belief/desire pair>) entails Q.

The explanation can then be formulated as follows. (For convenience, we treat CONJ as if it took n-tuples of propositions and returned "their conjunction.")

How should the *infinitistic* Weak Deflationist reply to Gupta? The instances of (ES) express explanations that focus on the property of truth and the relation of entailment, and not on whatever particular propositions are special to the conclusion. But is that not what is distinctive of explanations of general facts?[14] I submit that such explanation forms provide acceptable surrogates for explanations of the corresponding general facts. Horwich's explanation of Bill's success in getting a beer clues us to an acceptable surrogate for an explanation of (Success).

Weak Deflationism, then, whether finitistic or infinitistic, need not stumble over the explanation of general facts. I do not claim to have shown that Weak

1. For all P, Q, x, CONJ(<x believes IF(P, Q)>, <IF(P, Q) is true>, <x wants Q>, <x brings about P because...>) entails CONJ(<IF(P, Q) is true>, <x brings about P because...>)	Assm., fact of logic
2. For all P, Q, x, <x brings about P because...> entails P	Assm., unproblematic resource
3. For all P, Q, x, CONJ(IF(P, Q), <x brings about P because...>) entails Q	2, facts of logic
4. For all P, Q, x, CONJ(<IF(P, Q) is true>, <x brings about P because...>) entails Q	3, Wk. Defl.
5. For all P, Q, x, CONJ(<x believes IF(P, Q)>, <IF(P, Q) is true>, <x wants Q>, <x brings about P because...>) entails Q.	1, 4

[13] In fact, it seems that *if* the deflationist is entitled to employ a notion of material implication not explained in terms of truth, *then* there is a more general procedure that can be employed by finitistic Weak Deflationists for formulating explanations for general facts. This procedure is to be used when the general fact in need of explanation cannot be explained on the basis of the fact that some property is analyzable partly in terms of truth, but can be formulated by a sentence in prenex normal form in which the primary connective of the embedded open sentence is either the material conditional or material biconditional. The procedure is as follows.

Begin with a prenex sentence that expresses the general fact. Call this sentence EM (for "*explanandum*"). From EM, form its "propositional" equivalent, PEQ. This is done by first substituting, as is appropriate, the predicates 'materially implies' or 'is materially equivalent to' for the primary connective of the embedded open sentence, and then substituting appropriate singular terms referring to propositions for the (open) sentences flanking the main connective of the embedded sentence. Next, in PEQ, for every expression 'Tr(...)', substitute '...'. This leaves one with a sentence ES (for '*explanans*'). Finally, formulate the explanation of the general fact by constructing a derivation of EM from the premises ES and PEQ, together with a premise expressing an immediate consequence of Weak Deflationism and whatever unproblematic premises are needed. Here is simple illustration. The fact to be explained is the fact that for all P, Q, if CONJ(P, Q) is true, then P is true.

1. For all P, Q, CONJ(P, Q) materially implies P	(This is ES)	Assm., fact of logic
2. For all P, Tr(P) is necessarily equivalent to P		Assm., Wk. Defl.
3. For all P, Q, Tr(CONJ(P, Q)) materially implies Tr(P)	(This is PEQ)	1, 2
4. For all P, Q, if CONJ(P, Q) is true, then P is true.	(This is EM)	3, (PMI)

If necessary, the Weak Deflationist will need to provide additional premises to support ES.

[14] Here we are working with an intuitive notion of "general fact," which does not count facts expressed by sentences of the form 'Everyone who is identical to either a or b is F' as general.

Deflationism is adequate to explain all the general facts that need explaining, but only that the generality of such facts presents no problem for Weak Deflationism.

IV. DOES WEAK DEFLATIONISM HAVE THE RESOURCES TO EXPLAIN THE OBVIOUSNESS OF PROPOSITIONS EXPRESSED BY INSTANCES OF THE SCHEMA 'P' IS TRUE IFF P?

The obviousness of the propositions in question is a *datum* that any theory of truth must account for. Disquotationalists such as Quine take its obviousness to flow from the fact that "truth is disquotation." For the Weak Deflationist, though, truth for sentences is analyzed in such a way that instances of the disquotation schema do not directly follow.

Before trying to give an explanation, we need enlightenment on the *datum* we are being asked to explain. We are to explain the obviousness of propositions such as <'Snow is white' is true iff snow is white>. Obviousness to whom? Such propositions are not obvious to everyone. Knowledge of the *meaning* of 'Snow is white' should make it obvious that 'Snow is white' is true iff snow is white to anyone who has the concept of truth for sentences. So the task at hand for Weak Deflationism is to explain why it is that, for English sentence S, the proposition expressed by the S-instance of the disquotation schema will be obvious to those who know S's meaning and who have the concept of truth for sentences.

The Weak Deflationist discharges this task by offering the following schema:

(i) 'p' is true iff what 'p' expresses is true[15]	Assm., Wk. Defl.
(ii) p expresses <p>	Assm.
(iii) p is true iff <p> is true	(i), (ii)
(iv) <p> is true iff p	Assm., Wk. Defl.
(v) p is true iff p	(iii), (iv)

The Weak Deflationist claims that the propositions expressed by instances of (i) and (iv) will be obvious to anyone who has the concepts needed to entertain them. (i) is the schematic correlate of her *analysis* of truth for sentences, and (iv) expresses a form any instance of which follows from her account of propositional truth. The propositions expressed by instances of (ii) *give* the meaning of English sentences, and so are obvious to those who understand those sentences.

The explanation of the obviousness of propositions expressed by the disquotation schema, then, is essentially this: to know the meaning of a sentence of English is to know the proposition expressed by the corresponding instance of (ii); those who know such a proposition for an English sentence, and have a grasp of truth for sentences and propositional truth as explained by Weak Deflationism, can proceed through an obvious series of deductive steps to arrive at knowledge of the proposi-

---

[15] (i) is equivalent to

(i) 'p' is true iff 'p' expresses a true proposition

on the assumption (which I am making) that acceptable fillings for 'p' express exactly one proposition.

tion expressed by the instance of the disquotation schema corresponding to the sentence. The claim is not that we English speakers *do* proceed through such steps, but only that we could so proceed should we have need. Thus, the knowledge that 'Snow is white' is true iff snow is white is readily available to those who know the meaning of 'Snow is white'.

I note, finally, that the finitistic Weak Deflationist may explain the general fact that every proposition expressed by an instance of the disquotation schema is obvious to whomever understands the corresponding English sentence and has a grasp of truth for sentences.[16]

V. Can the Weak Deflationist Answer the Standard Objection to Correspondence Theories that if Truth Consisted in Correspondence with the Facts, Knowing Something is True would Require an Absurd Comparison between Sentences (Utterances, Beliefs) and Facts?

The "absurd comparison" objection has become a standard, if elusive, objection against correspondence theories of truth. It has been voiced at different times by Davidson (1986) and Rorty (1980, p. 179), among others, though Davidson recently expressed (1990, p. 302) doubts its soundness.[17] Prior to having these doubts, Davidson writes:

---

[16] The general *explanandum* is this: For all sentences S, persons P, if P understands S and grasps truth for sentences, IFF(Tr(S), EXP(S))) is obvious to P. If the Weak Deflationist is allowed a truth-free notion of material implication, the thing is easily done in the manner specified in note 51. If she is not allowed such a relation, an explanation is formulatable as follows.

(1) For all P, if P grasps truth for sentences,   Wk. Defl.
    <For all S, S is true iff EXP(S) is true> is obvious to P.

(2) For all P, if <For all S, S is true iff EXP(S) is true>   Unprob. Res.
    is obvious to P and P understands S, then there is a
    Q such that Q = EXP(S) and IFF(Tr(S), Tr(Q)) is
    obvious to P.

(3) For all S, P, if IFF(Tr(S), Tr(Q)) is obvious to P,   Wk. Defl.
    so is IFF(Tr(S), Q)

(4) For all S, P if S understands S and S grasps truth   (1) - (3)
    for sentences, then IFF(Tr(S), EXP(S)) is obvious to P.

The defense of (2) is as follows. If <For all S, S is true iff EXP(S) is true> is obvious to P, then P understands S, then there is a Q such that P knows with respect to Q that it is EXP(S). Given this knowledge, P has available to him the following obvious piece of reasoning: given that EXP(S) = Q and that for all S, S is true iff EXP(S) is true, S is true iff Q is true. Thus, IFF(Tr(S), Tr(Q)) is obvious to P.

[17] For Davidson's doubts, see Davidson (1990, p. 302). For sketches of the "absurd confrontations" objection, see Davidson (1986) and Rorty (1979), p. 179.

> If meanings are given by objective truth conditions there is a question how we can know that the conditions are satisfied, for this would appear to require a confrontation between what we believe and reality; and the idea of such a confrontation is absurd. (1986, p. 307)

The best I can make of the argument behind this sort of objection is this: if the correspondence theory is correct and the truth of something consists in its relation to some object or fact in the world, then to know that something is true we would need to be able to (directly) compare it to some object or fact in the world; but we never have (direct) access to objects or fact, and so we cannot carry out any such (direct) comparison; so if the correspondence theory is correct, we cannot know that anything is true; we do have such knowledge; so the correspondence theory is not correct.

The objection, as I have stated it, applies to correspondence theories of any and all kinds of truth, propositional truth, sentential truth, truth of beliefs, *etc*. Since Weak Deflationism gives a correspondence theory only for truth-bearers that express propositions, the objection does not apply against the theory of propositional truth, but only in the cases of sentential truth, attitudinal truth, *etc*. The objection derives its impetus, in any case, from the conviction that the idea of (directly) comparing a mental entity—belief, idea, thought—or an expression of a mental entity, a sentence or utterance—with a non-mental entity is incoherent. Propositions are neither mental entities nor expressions thereof.

What force does the objection have, then, against Weak Deflationism? Davidson doubts the soundness of the objection because, as he puts it, it "depends on assuming that some form of epistemic theory [of truth] is correct," and so would be a legitimate objection "only if truth were an epistemic concept" (1990, pp. 302-3). But it seems legitimate to require of a philosophical account of truth, or of almost any important property, that when conjoined with very basic epistemological principles that enjoy general acceptance, it not have the consequence that we cannot know about anything that it has the property. This is a very weak requirement on philosophical accounts. One might wish to require of such accounts that when conjoined with accepted epistemological principles, they imply no more and no less knowledge involving the property than we intuitively believe we have. But even if we work with the former, weaker requirement, we can see that the "absurd comparison" view is not properly dismissed simply because it depends on some general epistemic principles. Davidson seems to think the objection depends on an epistemic theory of truth. But let us see if the objection can work without making that assumption, by employing plausible epistemological principles.

It is not easy to identify a plausible epistemological principle to fit the bill. One principle that would suffice, it seems, is the principle that if property A analyzes property B, then to know that something has B one has to independently determine that it has A and then infer that it has B.[18] This principle, however, is too strong.

---

[18] Note that this principle depends on a view of analysis according to which if A analyzes B, A is not the same property as B.

An analysis of a property does not, at least in the first instance, aim to identify conditions knowledge of which we must bring to bear in justifying beliefs about the property's instantiation. Often there are no such conditions. Consider, for instance, content properties such as *having a thought about chocolate*. In one's own case, one does not (nor does one need to) employ as a inferential basis a piece of knowledge of special conditions distinct from the condition that one is having a thought about chocolate. Yet this does not rule out of court analyses of content properties. Again, consider the property of causality. In some cases, we employ knowledge of regularities in arriving at knowledge of causality, in other cases we do not, say in the case of one's immediate perception of the impact of one's decisions on one's limbs. But this is no reason to think causality is unanalyzable.

Even if we disregard the above considerations, though, we can see that the "absurd comparison" objection has no force against Weak Deflationism, for a simple reason. Under Weak Deflationism, anyone equipped with the concepts of truth for sentences (beliefs, utterances) who knows the content of a sentence (belief, utterance) its corresponding truth-equivalence is obvious. This was shown in the preceding section in connection with sentences. Anyone who knows the meaning of 'Snow is white', has easy access to the knowledge that 'Snow is white' is true iff snow is white. Thus, merely by looking at snow, one who knows the meaning of 'Snow is white' may discover the truth-value of the sentence. No comparison between the sentence and the world is needed. Similarly, no one who knows the content of his thought that it is snowing needs to compare his thought to the world; he is guaranteed of knowing that his thought is true iff it is snowing. *Mutatis mutandis* for utterances. Correspondence, under Weak Deflationism, is a matter not of similarity between truth-bearer and fact, whether intrinsic or extrinsic, but of the truth of the proposition expressed. And since truth for propositions is deflationary, one who grasps propositional truth knows that for any proposition *P*, finding out *P* is finding out that *P* is true, and vice versa.

The concerns motivating the "absurd comparison" objection are perhaps more productively aimed against certain brands of epistemic foundationalism. The principle that the *relata* of justification relations must be possessed of propositional content, for example, might be used to undermine a foundationalist view according to which justification of empirical beliefs ultimately rests upon sense-data or experiences, conceived as lacking content.

VI. Is Weak Deflationism Incompatible with Non-Factualist Theories of Certain Areas of Declarative Discourse, e.g., Moral Discourse?

My answer to this question will be "no." I will try to show that although deflationism about sentential truth conflicts with non-factualist theses, a Weak Deflationist may consistently formulate non-factualism theses within the framework of Weak Deflationism using the notion of *expression of a proposition*.

Paul Boghossian (1990) has argued that deflationism cannot be squared with non-factualism about any range of declarative discourse. This, he claims, is devastating to deflationism, since in his estimation deflationism itself is a non-factualist thesis about sentences involving the predicate 'is true'. I concentrate of this first thesis, since the second depends on the first. If the first is undercut, the second is as well.

Boghossian characterizes deflationism as the thesis that there is no such thing as the property of truth, a property that sentences or thoughts may enjoy, and that would be named by the words 'true' or 'truth'. (1990, p. 161). Right away, then, we see a problem. Weak Deflationism, like Horwich's minimalism, recognizes a property of truth, and yet is rightly called deflationist insofar as it characterizes propositional truth in terms of the simple form <<p> is true iff p>. The *property* of truth is deflated. But perhaps Boghossian's criticisms can be extended to theories such as Weak Deflationism. So let us see what he means by saying 'true' does not express a property. He claims 'true' expresses a property iff there are normal declarative sentences that are *not* truth-apt. In other words, if truth-aptitude is not selective between declarative sentences, 'true' fails to express a property. Being a normal declarative sentence is a matter of "of coherent embedding within negation, the conditional, and other connectives, and within contexts of propositional attitude." (1990, p. 163). Deflationism then becomes the thesis that all normal declarative sentences are truth-apt. To extend the account to propositions, we might say: a 'that'-clause ⌈that-S⌉ expresses a truth-apt proposition iff S is truth-apt.

If Boghossian is right, deflationists must regard the moral sentence 'Kicking dogs is wrong' as true or false and the 'that'-clause 'that kicking dogs is wrong' as expressive of a true or false proposition. This would entail the rejection of moral non-factualism by consistent deflationists who do not wish to take an error-theoretic approach to moral discourse. The disadvantages of an error theory of moral discourse are inhibiting: one would have to regard moral language as in the business of stating truths but failing; as a result, it would seem difficult to fully embrace moral talk with knowledge of its true status—one would be embracing the regular production of false assertions.

But why should a deflationist admit that aptitude for truth is a matter of coherent embedding? Why think that a deflationist approach to 'true' implies, let alone consists in, a latitudinarian approach to truth-aptitude? Consider this remark by Crispin Wright:

> ...it is essential to deflationism—its most basic and distinctive contention—
> that 'true' is merely a device of endorsing assertions...(Wright 1992, p. 33)

On Wright's view, deflationism's leading claim is that by asserting "'S' is true"(or to be precise, the English sentence formed by appending 'is true' to a quote name of S) it is *as if* one has *merely* asserted S itself. Latitudinarianism of truth-aptitude is then immediately forthcoming from deflationism, for any well-behaved declarative sentence will meet the condition specified: if in asserting "'Snow is white' is true" it is as if one has merely asserted 'Snow is white', then surely in asserting "'Kicking dogs is wrong' is true" it is no less the case that it is as if one has merely asserted 'Kicking dogs is wrong'. What could justify a dividing line? One is led to think that in asserting "'Snow is white' is true" it is as if one asserts 'Snow is white' because the former assertion carries with it all the assertive commitments of the latter and vice versa. Thus, whether one asserts "'Snow is white' is true" or 'Snow is white', one is committed to asserting, *e.g.*, 'Snow is not red', and one is committed to inferring, *e.g.*, from the assertion 'Clinton said that snow is white' the assertion 'Clinton said something true'. The same goes for 'Kicking dogs is wrong'. Thus, it seems that if Wright—and Boghossian—are right in linking deflationism with the claim that in asserting "'S' is true" it is as if one asserts S itself, then latitudinarianism about truth-aptitude is unavoidable for the deflationist.

However, as we have seen, a deflationist about truth for sentences has good reason to take S and "'S' is true" to express different propositions. S need not be about a sentence, while "'S' is true" plainly is. Even so, it seems to me that Wright and Boghossian might be able to make their essential point simply by reference to the disquotation schema. If truth for sentences is explained by reference to this schema, in the manner discussed earlier in this chapter, the question arises how one could justify counting moral sentences and other "problematic" declarative sentences as inadmissible substitutends for '*p*'.

I submit that deflationists about truth for sentences cannot provide an adequate answer to this question. To follow Jackson, Oppy, and Smith (1994) and Smith (1994) in claiming that truth-aptitude is one thing, truth another is no answer, as I now will show. Jackson, Oppy and Smith begin by pointing out, quite rightly, that although deflationists explain truth for sentences by reference to the disquotation schema, deflationism does not thereby imply that all well-behaved English declarative sentences are admissible substitutends for the schematic letter '*p*', and so nor does it imply that all normal English declarative sentences are apt for truth. Jackson, Oppy, and Smith write:

> Why should anyone think that minimalism about truth... leads pretty well directly to the falsity of non-cognitivism...?...
> The answer favoured by Horwich (1993, 73-4) is that minimalism about truth means that the appropriate substitutions in the T-schema:
> (T) '*p*' is true iff *p*
> deliver truth conditions...for ethical sentences...Thus, substituting in (T), we might get:
> (1) 'Torture is wrong' is true iff torture is wrong.
> So the argument runs, 'Torture is wrong' has a truth condition, and is thereby truth-apt.
> There is an obvious problem with this argument. Granted, *if* (1) gave the condition under which 'Torture is wrong' is true, it would follow that 'Torture is wrong' is truth apt. But (1) only does that if its right-hand side is truth apt, and *that* is the question. (Jackson, Oppy and Smith 1994, pp. 288-9).

Yes. But there remains a question for deflationism. If one explains truth for sentences in terms of the disquotation schema while maintaining the distinctness of the question of which declarative sentences are admissible substitutions, the question arises why aptitude for *truth* should fail among some but not all declarative sentences. Jackson, Oppy, and Smith's answer, that aptitude for truth is analytically linked with aptitude for expressing belief (1994, pp. 294), only raises the question of why aptitude for truth and aptitude for expressing belief should be linked. This is a question about truth. It is this: What is it about *truth* such that aptitude for it requires aptitude for expressing belief?

It is important here that the notion of belief to which appeal is being made is non-minimalist.[19] There is no definitional guarantee, from the fact that a sentence is a well-behaved declarative sentence that it expresses a belief. Belief is a state of mind defined, as Searle says, in terms of its direction of fit, a direction not shared by desires. Beliefs have the proper function of fitting themselves with the world, desires of fitting the world with them. A belief that p tends to go out of existence in the presence of a perception that not-p, while a desire that p does not and in fact remains in existence, motivating the subject to bring it about that p. (Smith 1987, p. 54). This, of course, rules out only the possibility that a belief that p could be a desire that p, not the possibility that a belief that p could be a desire that q. The question arises, then, of whether a desire that, *ceteris paribus*, dogs not be kicked—or something of the sort—is a belief that kicking dogs is wrong. One way to defend a negative answer is to appeal to Humeanism about belief: the mere possession of a belief provides no motivation. In any case, the deflationist who follows Jackson, Oppy, and Smith is in need of such a non-minimalist account of belief.

The Weak Deflationist, who rejects deflationism about sentential truth, has a reply to the question 'What is it about *truth* such that aptitude for it requires aptitude for expressing belief?': truth for sentences consists in the expression of true propositions; but not all sentences express propositions, only those that are apt for expressing belief (against construed in non-minimalist terms). The deflationist about truth for sentences cannot make this reply. It is unclear to me what reply she can offer other than to insist that truth-aptitude is analytically connected to the expression of belief. But if aptitude for *truth* bears this analytic connection to expression of belief, then *truth*, too, bears to it an analytic connection, and the explanation of this analytic connection imports something substantial into what was assumed to be a deflationist account of truth for sentences. Smith (1994) himself recognizes this point:

> (M)inimalism about truth in fact *presupposes* a psychological theory, a theory whose concepts of belief and desire will in turn constrain which sentences can and cannot count as truth-assessable. But if minimalism presupposes a psychological theory then, given that a psychological theory is a substantive theory about the way human beings work, it follows that minimalism itself requires substantive assumptions in giving accounts of truth and truth-assessability after all. (1994, p. 8)

Calling a connection analytic, however, does not relieve one of the responsibility of illuminating it. Jackson, Oppy, and Smith label as analytic any connection between properties P and Q that is *a priori* and obvious to all grasp P and Q (1994, p. 294).

---

[19] See Divers and Miller (1994), however, for a minimalist account of belief.

Thus, it would be analytic, presumably, that if event *c* causes event *e*, then there is some law *L* that covers this interaction and that if something is known, it is true. These, however, are facts for which we should demand an explanation in terms of a philosophical account of the relevant property, causality and knowledge. The deflationist is not exempted from this general requirement in her invocation of the connection between aptitude for truth and aptitude for expression of belief. Merely listing the platitudes surrounding a concept is not analyzing the concept; an analysis *unifies* platitudes, thereby illuminating them.

The main point of all this is that for the Weak Deflationist there is no reason to think the analytic connection between truth for sentences and the expression of belief is unexplainable. For, truth for sentences consists in expression of a true proposition, a notion itself to be understood in terms of the expression of belief. The deflationist about sentential truth, on the other hand, seems to have nowhere to turn: it must be taken as given that truth for sentences bears an analytic connection to the expression of belief.

My aim has not been to resolve debates between non-factualists and factualists concerning moral talk, or any other variety of declarative talk, but only to show that Weak Deflationism provides a neutral framework within which these discussions can be pursued; it neither rules in nor rules out non-factualist theses about particular areas of declarative discourse.

Boghossian's argument, I conclude, does indirectly raise difficulties for deflationists who wish not to rule out non-factualist theories from the start, but these difficulties do not touch Weak Deflationism.

VII. Why Can't We Use Higher-Order Quantification to Formulate Deflationism about Propositional Truth as a Universalized Biconditional?

Mark Eli Kalderon (1997) has suggested that deflationism about propositional truth might be formulated as follows:

(K) For all x, x is true iff there is a p such that x = the proposition that p and p

where 'x' is a first-order variable and 'p' is a higher-order variable that has the same range as 'x'. The sentential variable 'p', in other words, is given an objectual reading. If 'p' were understood substitutionally, (K) would be inadequate, either because it is circular or because it is expressively inadequate (owing to the expressive limitations of English). Our question, then, is whether (K) can be interpreted as an objectual higher-order quantification.

What is it for a variable to be objectual? It is not enough to say, "It is for objects to be assignable to it." For we want to know what it is for a variable to count as having objects assigned to it. Standardly, first-order quantification is explained as follows:

'For all x, Fx' is true under interpretation I iff for every interpretation I^* just like I except possibly in the object o assigned to 'x', 'Fx' is true under I^*.

'Fx' is true under interpretation I iff the object I assigns to 'x' is a member of the extension of 'F'.

Since we are concerned with natural language, or more precisely, a philosopher's extension thereof (including 'x', 'y',..., 'F', 'G',... 'p', 'q' as variables), we may bypass reference to interpretations. What we want is a schema for translating the philosopher's higher-order sentences into ordinary English. We may in fact think of the philosopher's extension of English as a more perspicuous language than ordinary English albeit one with the same expressive powers. The following translation scheme for the philosopher's *first*-order quantification seems reasonable:

'For all x, x is F' is translated as 'Every object is F'.
'For some x, x is F' is translated as 'Some object is F'.

The sense in which first-order variables are objectual is then this: a first-order quantified sentence attributes to objects in the domain of the variable the condition specified in the sentence. Thus, 'For all x, x is a dog' attributes to every object in the domain of 'x' the property of being a dog.

This understanding of the objectuality of first-order variables gives us a plausible account of objectuality of variables in general: a variable is objectual iff quantified sentences containing it as the sole variable attribute to objects in the variable's domain the condition specified in the sentence. Objectual higher-order variables, if there are any, would differ from their first-order counterparts only in that they range exclusively over properties (propositions). Understanding objectuality in this way, can we understand higher-order quantification as objectual? Consider these higher-order sentences:

For all F, Bill Clinton is F.

For all p, p.

Can we understand these as attributing to objects in their variables' domains specified conditions? How should we replace the dots in the following?

'For all F, Bill Clinton is F' is translated as 'Every property meets the condition that it...'

'For all p, p' is translated as 'Every proposition meets the condition that it...'

The natural replacements are these:

'For all F, Bill Clinton is F' is translated as 'Every property meets the condition that it *is exemplified by Bill Clinton*'

'For all p, p' is translated as 'Every proposition meets the condition that it *is true*'

I do not see any other alternatives.[20]

---

[20] My doubts about the use of higher-order quantification to analyze truth or exemplification are similar to Herbert Heidelberger's. Cf. Heidelberger on "stray variables,"in Heidelerger (1968), especially pp. 214-5. Thanks to James van Cleve for making me aware of this similarity.

The philosopher's higher-order quantification using sentential variables (predicate variables) is objectual, it seems, only if understood in terms of truth (exemplification). Thus, such quantification cannot be used in formulating deflationism about truth and exemplification. For consider the translations of Kalderon's (K) and its cousin for exemplification:

> 'For all x, x is true iff there is a p such that x = the proposition that p & p' is translated as 'Every proposition is such that it is true iff there is a proposition to which it is identical and which is true'.

> 'For all x, F, x exemplifies F-ness iff x is F' is translated as 'Every object is such that, for any property, the object exemplifies the property iff the object exemplifies the property'.

These are small circles indeed. Deflationism about propositional truth and about property exemplification resist formulation in terms of higher-order quantification.

CHAPTER 4

A Challenge from David Lewis

Let us use 'Platonism' to denote the following thesis about properties and propositions.[1]

(Platonism)

(About Properties)

There are properties. Properties are abstract. Some properties are simples. Simple properties are not sets. Properties that are not simples have simple properties as constituents.

(About Propositions)

There are propositions. If they are simples, they are abstracta but not sets. If they are not simples, they are complexes having properties as constituents.

I characterize Platonism in this broad way to allow for Platonists who differ on the details, e.g., whether *all* properties are simples, whether propositions are simples or complexes.[2] What unifies Platonists is the belief that properties and propositions are, or have as constituents, simple abstracta that are not sets. This distinguishes Platonism about properties from nominalism (including linguistic, class, resemblance, and trope nominalisms)[3] and from what might be called Aristotelianism, the proponents of which deny that properties are abstract, claiming that a property

---

[1] I use 'property' here in a broad sense to denote relations as well as monadic properties. For the most part, though, I will focus my discussion on monadic properties.

[2] A Platonist might even believe that there are Russellian propositions, propositions that have among their constituents concrete objects. Acceptance of Russellian propositions is consistent with Platonism, so long as 'abstract' is understood in a broad sense under which having an abstract object as a constituent suffices for being abstract.

exists only if instantiated, only if "fully present" in instances.[4] Platonism about propositions is distinguished, not only from eliminativism about propositions, but from views that identify propositions with sets of concreta, *e.g.*, the view that propositions are sets of relevantly similar utterances. Adherents of Platonism in recent philosophy include Alvin Plantinga (1973, 1987), Roderick Chisholm (1996), and George Bealer (1993).

If Platonism is true, then in keeping with the arguments of previous chapters, property exemplification and propositional truth are unanalyzable. The reason is this. Any adequate analysis of exemplification (truth) would need to provide the resources for deriving instances of the following equivalence schema for exemplification (truth), 'For all x, necessarily, x exemplifies F-ness iff x is F' ('Necessarily, <p> is true iff p').[5] [6] But given a candidate *analysans* condition, R-ing, for exemplification, it would seem to be unexplainable why the fact that a thing Rs the Platonic property, *whiteness*, should insure its being white, and vice versa; and given any candidate *analysans* condition, G-ness, for truth, it would seem to be unexplainable why the fact that the Platonic proposition, <The coffee is hot>, is G should insure the coffee's being hot, and vice versa.

Enter now the concrete modal realist. She offers a two-part challenge to Platonism. Concrete modal realism, she first claims, has the advantage over Platonism that it is equipped to deliver *analysantia* conditions for truth and exemplification. All the trouble we have encountered in formulating the Weak Deflationist theory of propositional truth (exemplification) and showing how the theory could explain general facts about truth (exemplification) could be painlessly avoided. Second, relying on a dilemma posed by Lewis, she argues that truth and exemplification under Platonism are unintelligible.

I reply on behalf of the Platonist, and in particular, on behalf of the Platonist who accepts Weak Deflationism about exemplification and truth, whom I will call the *Deflationist Platonist*. As a deflationist, the Deflationist Platonist claims that the simple exemplification and truth equivalences are constitutive of exemplification and truth. As we have seen, several options are open to the Weak Deflationist in formulating accounts of truth and exemplification. In this chapter, let us consider the

---

[3] See Armstrong (1978).

[4] For discussion of Aristotelianism, see Armstrong (1993) and Lewis (1984).

[5] These constraints on theories of exemplification and truth may need to be modified, for two reasons. First, faced with liar-like phenomena, we might wish to reject some instances of the equivalence schemata. Second, some realists about properties (propositions) might deny that each meaningful, non-paradoxical predicate (sentence) expresses a property (proposition). So we might wish to specify in our statement of the constraints that the substitution class of predicate expressions (sentences) is restricted to those that express properties (propositions).

[6] One might suppose it legitimate to require only the deliverance of the equivalences and not the attributions of necessity. But we may ask: What would it be for something to be red but not exemplify redness? What would it be for something to exemplify redness but not be red? If there is a property of redness, it is a matter of necessity that it is exemplified by something just in case it is red. *Mutatis mutandis* for truth.

following formulations, which invoke *a priori* necessary explanation relations that may hold between properties and between propositions:[7]

For all properties Φ, Φ explains the property of exemplifying Φ

For all propositions P, P explains the proposition that P is true.[8]

The Deflationist Platonist claims that all the facts involving exemplification and truth, or at least all that require explanation, can be explained on the basis of these simple theories.[9] In particular, she claims that the exemplification and truth equivalences are readily obtainable from her account, given the unproblematic schemata

If F-ness explains G-ness, then, for any x, necessarily, x is F iff x is G

If <p> explains <q>, then, <p> and <q> are necessarily equivalent

If <p> entails <q>, then if p, then q. [This is the inference rule (PE) discussed in previous chapters.]

where 'explains', as figures in these schemata, is understood as expressing the appropriate *a priori* necessary explanation relations. The guiding thought of Deflationist Platonism is that facts about the exemplification of properties and the truth of propositions are accounted for by the ground level facts, which are exemplification-free and truth-free (and free of all other truth-like properties such as *being false of* and falsity). The fact that snow is white accounts for both the fact that snow exemplifies whiteness and the fact that the proposition that snow is white is true. The ground level facts account for *all* other facts. To illustrate the simplest sort of case: each of the facts in the series

---

[7] My use of 'explains' here is special. See Chapter 2, pp. 32-3 for detailed discussion. Here I give a brief summary. The explanation relations invoked by Deflationist Platonism resemble explanation relations holding—or alleged to hold by certain Fregeans—, respectively, between properties Φ and ψ just in case Φ analyzes ψ, and between propositions P and Q just in case P and Q are alike except for the fact that whereas P involves an attribution of a property Φ, Q involves an attribution of its *analysans* property, ψ. So, if we found that justified true belief analyses knowledge, we could say that the former *explains* the latter; we might also say that <Bob Dole believes truly and with justification that he won the election> *explains* <Bob Dole knows that he won the election>. Note that these explanations relations hold independently of whether their *relata (relatum)* are exemplified (true). Compare: being a round square *explains* the property of exemplifying being a round square; <Muddy water is clear> *explains* <<Muddy water is clear> is true>. The use of the subjunctive makes for better English: what it *would* be for something to exemplify being a round square *would* be for it to be a round square; what it *would* be for <Muddy water is clear> to be true *would* be for muddy water to be clear.

[8] The schematic expressions 'the property of exemplifying P' and 'the proposition that P is true' must be given Russellian readings. Thus, these are read, respectively, as short for 'the property with respect to P of exemplifying it' and 'the proposition with respect to P that it is true'.

Again, I am bracketing concerns about the liar-like paradoxes. See Chapter 6.

[9] This requirement on theories of truth can be found in Horwich (1990, p. 7).

> The fact that <Snow is white> is true
>
> The fact that <<Snow is white> is true> is true
>
> The fact that <<<Snow is white> is true> is true> is true
>
> ...

is accounted for by the fact that snow is white.

I. THE FIRST PART OF THE CHALLENGE

Perhaps theories presupposing concrete modal realism are best met with what Lewis calls "the incredulous stare," and a prompt dismissal (Lewis 1986, p. 133). Concrete modal realism, after all, affirms the existence of cats that are molecule-for-molecule duplicates of our pets but which are spatio-temporally unrelated to them; these otherworldly cats really exist, but they are parts of other spatio-temporal systems. Moreover, and more incredibly, the states of some otherwordly cats—those whose similarity to our cats qualifies them as *counterparts* of our cats—underwrite *de re* possibilities for our cats (Lewis 1986, p. 89). A host of questions arise: Why aren't cats spatio-temporally unrelated to us and our pets still parts of actuality? What qualifies spatio-temporal relatedness as the worldmate-determining relation? How does the mere existence of a three-legged cat similar, but spatio-temporally unrelated, to my cat ground the *de re* possibility that my cat is three-legged?

The concrete modal realist might reply, as Lewis does, by saying that concrete worlds "earn their keep." I think we may agree that it would be a mark in favor of any philosophical view, so long as it is consistent with our empirical knowledge, that if it were true, it would provide the materials for simple, non-arbitrary analyses of truth and exemplification. What I will argue, however, in this first section of this essay, is that concrete modal realism does not provide the necessary materials. Even if properties and propositions are what the concrete modal realist says they are, truth and exemplification are not analyzable. Lewis's paradise of a *plenum* of concrete worlds, for all its richness, is too poor.

Let us turn, then, to the concrete modal realist theories in question. Worlds, for Lewis, are maximal mereological sums of spatio-temporally related entities. They are maximal in the sense that the parts of worlds are spatio-temporally related to one another and no world has a part that is spatio-temporally related to anything that is not likewise a part of that world. Propositions are identified with sets of such worlds, and properties with sets of parts of such worlds (with *possibilia*). (Since worlds themselves are parts of worlds, propositions turn out to constitute a species of property, properties whose instances are all and only worlds (Lewis 1986, p. 53-4).) What I call the concrete modal realist theory of properties is thus a version of class nominalism.

With this machinery in place, the concrete modal realist may formulate candidate analyses of truth and exemplification:

(1) For all propositions P, worlds W, P is true at W iff $W \in P$

(2) For all properties Φ, entities x, and worlds W, x exemplifies Φ at W iff x is part of W and $x \in \Phi$

These candidate analyses are genuine analyses only if the truth and exemplification equivalences, respectively, are obtainable from them, together with unproblematic principles. Although, as far as I know, Lewis does not draw attention to it, it appears that if the concrete modal realist theories of properties and propositions are assumed, the desired equivalences are forthcoming.

We begin with the case of truth. From (1), using 'α' to tag the actual world, we may obtain

(3) For all propositions P, P is true at α iff $\alpha \in P$

From (3), together with the schema

(4) $<p>$ = $\{u: \text{at world } u, p\}$[10]

we may obtain

(5) $<p>$ is true at α iff $\alpha \in \{u: \text{at world } u, p\}$

Given (5), we may use the principle of set abstraction—the principle that for all x, $x \in \{y: Fy\}$ iff Fx—to obtain

(6) $<p>$ is true at α iff at α, p

Letting the actuality operators go implicit, we have the truth equivalences

(7) $<p>$ is true iff p

Moreover, since the instances of (7) hold at every world, we arrive at

(8) Necessarily, $<p>$ is true iff p

The exemplification equivalences are obtainable, in similar fashion, from (2). In place of (4), we use

(9) F-ness = $\{x: x \text{ is } F\}$

From (2) and (9), we may obtain

(10) For all x, x exemplifies F-ness at α iff x is part of α and, in α, x is F

Letting the references to actuality go implicit, we have the exemplification equivalences:

(11) For all x, x exemplifies F-ness iff x is F

---

[10] This schema would perhaps need to be modified to accommodate the fact that individuals (for Lewis) exist in at most one world. Consider the proposition that Bill Clinton is tall. This proposition is not identical with the set of worlds at which Bill Clinton himself is tall, but rather with the set of worlds at which Bill Clinton or some counterpart of his is tall. However, I trust no essential point will be neglected if we employ the simpler (4).

Given counterpart theory, instances of (11) give way to instances

(12) For all x, necessarily, x exemplifies F-ness iff x is F

Concrete modal realism thus provides the tools for accounts of truth and exemplification that are genuine candidates for analyses. (1) and (2) are closed universalized biconditionals specifying unitary conditions that pairs of propositions and worlds and triples of individuals, properties, and worlds must meet, respectively, for the proposition to be true at the world and for the individual to exemplify the property at the world. Thus, (1) and (2) would enable us to *define* 'true at w' and 'exemplifies at w': 'x is true at world w' =df '$w \in x$'; 'x exemplifies y at world w' =df 'x is a part of w & $x \in y$'. Moreover, (1) and (2), together with the concrete modal realist principles concerning the identity of properties and propositions, yield the exemplification and truth equivalences. So, what is to stop us from considering (1) and (2) genuine analyses of truth and exemplification, if we put to one side concerns over ontological parsimony and the adequacy of counterpart relations for the grounding of modality?

A short and incisive, but ultimately unconvincing, argument threatens these proposed analyses, charging them with circularity. The argument is prompted by Lewis's remarks in passages such as this one:

> I identify propositions with certain properties—namely, with those that are instantiated only by entire possible worlds. Then if properties generally are the sets of their instances, a proposition is a set of possible worlds. A proposition is said to *hold* at a world, or to be *true at* a world. The proposition is the same thing as the property of being a world where that proposition holds; and that is the same thing as the set of worlds where that proposition holds. (1986, p. 53-54)

Here Lewis puts forth the following principles:

(13) For all propositions P, P = {u: at u, P is true}

(14) For all properties Φ, Φ = {i: i exemplifies Φ}

The complaint is this. In the presence of (13) and (14), we can reformulate (1) by (15), which is formed from (1) by replacing P with {u: at u, P is true} .

(15) For all propositions P, worlds W, P is true at W iff $W \in$ {u: at u, P is true}

But (15) gives us a very small circle, and so no analysis of truth. It says: a proposition is true at a world just in case the world is a member of the set of worlds at which the proposition is true. For analogous reasons, the corresponding reformulation of (2) will not do as an analysis of exemplification:

(16) For all properties Φ, entities x, and worlds W, x exemplifies Φ at W iff x is part of W and $x \in$ {i: i exemplifies Φ}

(16) says: a property is exemplified by an object at a world iff the object is part of the world and the object is a member of the set of things that exemplify the property. But if (15) and (16) are not analyses, neither are mere reformulations, (1) and (2).

This argument fails. It assumes that insofar as Lewis believes (13) and (14), he must treat (15) and (16) as mere reformulations of his analyses of truth and exemplification. What we have is a case in which substitution of co-referring terms turns an analytic claim to a non-analytic claim. If (13) and (14) were intended as *explanatory* of the notions of proposition and property, we would perhaps have grounds for complaint, for in that case, the substitutions in question would seem to preserve analytic status. But I submit that the way to think of (13) and (14), for Lewis, is as trivial rather than as explanatory truths, trivial because they are immediate consequences of his proposed analyses of exemplification and truth. If it is analytic that a proposition P is true at world W iff $W \in P$, then trivially, a proposition P is the set of the worlds at which it is true. If it is analytic that an individual x exemplifies a property Φ at world W iff x is part of W and $x \in \Phi$, then trivially, a property Φ is the set of individuals that exemplify it.

Another line of attack targets the principles (4) and (9), used in the derivations of the exemplification and truth equivalences:

(4) $<p> = \{u: \text{at world } u, p\}$

(9) $F\text{-ness} = \{x: x \text{ is } F\}$

Both principles are problematic. They yield, respectively, the schemata

(17) $<p> = <q>$ iff, at every world, p iff q

(18) $F\text{-ness} = G\text{-ness}$ iff, at every world, for all x, x is F iff x is G

These will not do, for familiar reasons. As Lewis acknowledges, propositions are the sorts of things that serve as contents of propositional attitudes (Lewis 1986, p. 55). But if (17) were correct, there would be one necessary proposition and one impossible proposition, so that $<2+2=4>$ and $<\text{Water is H}_2\text{O}>$ would be one and the same proposition, as would $<2+2=5>$ and $<\text{Water is not H}_2\text{O}>$. But one can obviously believe $<2+2=4>$ without believing $<\text{Water is H}_2\text{O}>$, and one can obviously believe $<\text{Water is not H}_2\text{O}>$ without believing $<2+2=5>$. Lewis might try adding structure to propositions, perhaps construing propositions as ordered sequences of objects and properties, the properties still being construed as unstructured sets of individuals. But properties themselves are essentially the sorts of things that can figure in the contents of *de re* propositional attitudes. If (18) were correct, it would follow that to believe, with respect to a face of a pyramid, that it is triangular is just to believe, with respect to it, that it is trilateral. This is clearly incorrect.

Lewis is resourceful in responding to these worries. He assures us that those who demand finely individuated properties can be placated by the recognition of structured properties, properties that are built set-theoretically from other properties. Perhaps, for example, we need to invoke both structured and unstructured properties of triangularity and trilaterality, the structured properties being distinct and the unstructured properties identical.

> Let A be the relation of being an angle of; let S be the relation of being a side of. Suppose for simplicity that these can be left as unstructured relations; we could go to a deeper level of analysis if we like, but that would complicate the construction without showing anything new. Let T be the higher-order unstruc-

tured relation which holds between an unstructured property F of individuals and an unstructured relation G of individuals iff F is the property of being something which exactly three things bear relation G to. A certain unstructured property is the unique thing which bears T to A, and therefore it is the (unstructured) property of triangularity; it also is the unique thing which bears T to S, and therefore it is the (unstructured) property of trilaterality. Therefore let us take the structured property of triangularity as the pair <T, A>, and the structured property of trilaterality as the pair <T, S>. Since S and A differ, we have the desired difference between the two pairs that we took to be our structured properties. (Lewis, 1986, pp. 56-7)

The technique is artificial, but it seems to give us the differences we seek. One notable presupposition is required, however, if the account is to work: no two ultimate unstructured properties are necessarily coextensive. Unstructured properties are distinct just if they differ in membership.[11]

This presupposition might seem to render Lewis's account vulnerable. For consider the determinable properties *being shaped* and *being extended*. These do not appear to be molecular properties, nor do they seem to have constituents in the way triangularity and trilaterality do. Yet they appear to be necessarily coextensive. Aren't they examples of necessarily equivalent unstructured properties? Perhaps not. Lewis might reply:

> *Being shaped* and *being extended* are second-order properties; *being shaped* is the second order property *having a shape*, and *being extended* is the second-order property *having an extension*. The properties *being a shape* and *being an extension* are themselves unstructured and distinct. Moreover, these properties are constitutively involved, respectively, in the properties *having a shape* and *having an extension*. There is a relation R such that R holds between an individual x and a property Φ just in case x has a property Γ and Γ has Φ. Thus, if apple A is round, then A stands in R to the property *being a shape*; and if A occupies space, then A stands in R to the property *being an extension*. So why not think of *being shaped* as <R, *being a shape*> and *being extended* as <R, *being an extension*>? To have *being shaped* is to stand in R to *being a shape*. To have *being extended* is to stand in R to *being an extension*.

In general, it appears that we may adequately accommodate the case of necessarily coextensive determinables by first construing them as second-order properties and then applying the above technique. I know of no other cases that present a serious challenge to Lewis's claim that he can distinguish any properties that need distinguishing simply using set-theoretical constructions from *possibilia*.

---

[11] Lewis *needs* unstructured properties. Consider the structured property of triangularity, <T, A>. To have <T, A> is *not* to be a member of it. Its members are properties, whereas <T, A> is a property of individuals. What it is for an object X to have <T, A>, it seems, is for the pair (X, A) to have T. But now if T, in turn, is structured, a pair's having T will consist in a triple's having of some three-place relation. And so the chain continues. Now, if there is *anything* it is for X to have <T, A>, this chain must come to an end. But it can end only at an n-tuple's having some unstructured n-ary relation. Exemplification of structured properties (relations) depends ultimately on exemplification of unstructured properties (relations).

If we are to find fault, we must look deeper. We must look to additional requirements we may legitimately impose on accounts of exemplification and truth. Consider the following sundry facts. If the lemon in my tea exemplifies tartness, then the fact that it is tart is explanatorily relevant to that exemplification-fact. But the fact that the numerically distinct lemon in your glass of tea is tart is not explanatorily relevant. This and similar examples motivate the following requirement on theories of exemplification:

(E) Where x exemplifies F-ness, an adequate theory of exemplification ought to be compatible with the claim that x has a unique explanatory status in respect of its exemplifying F-ness: x is the only thing such that the fact that it is F is explanatorily relevant to the fact that x exemplifies F-ness.[12][13]

---

[12] In (i) and (ii), the locution 'the fact that...is F' is used to form Russellian designators. It abbreviates the more cumbersome locution 'the fact with respect to...that it is F'. Lewis rejects the notion of facts as complexes the constituents of which are combined in some non-mereological fashion. Such a notion would allow for distinct facts composed of all the same constituents. The notion of fact required for my argument, however, is nothing more than that of a truth. 'Fact' as it occurs (E) should be interpreted to mean *truth*.

I thank a referee for raising possible counterexamples to (E). Consider Jewishness. Suppose S exemplifies Jewishness. It then seems that S's parents status as being Jewish is explanatorily relevant to S's exemplifying Jewishness. Consider dissective redness. If x exemplifies dissective redness, the redness of proper parts of x are explanatorily relevant to that fact.

Regarding Jewishness, we might restrict the range of 'F' to predicates expressing non-transmissible properties. Regarding dissective redness, we might reply the material following the colon with

nothing wholly disjoint from x is such that the fact that *it* is F is explanatorily relevant to the fact that x exemplifies F-ness.

Alternatively, we might propose a general amendment of (E) to handle both sorts of counterexamples. Following the colon, we might insert

nothing distinct from x is such that the fact that it is F is directly explanatorily relevant to the fact that x exemplifies F-ness.

The intuition here, which might need some elaboration, would be that even if there is some y distinct from x such that the fact that y is F is explanatorily relevant to the fact that x exemplifies F-ness, the explanatory route is indirect: y's being F is directly explanatorily relevant to x's being F, which in turn is directly explanatorily relevant to x's exemplifying F-ness.

I use (E) because I think it is plausible on its face. But for the purposes of my argument against Lewis, a weaker but stranger-sounding principle will do:

Where x exemplifies F-ness, an adequate theory of exemplification ought to be compatible with the following claims: (i) the fact that x is F is explanatorily relevant to the fact that x exemplifies F-ness; (ii) there is some y such that the fact that y is not F is not explanatorily relevant to the fact that x exemplifies F-ness.

Given (E), a theory of exemplification must not rule out the possibility that the lemon in my tea is unique in that its tartness matters, explanatorily, to the fact that the lemon in my tea exemplifies tartness. We can think of (E) epistemically as requiring that one's theory of exemplification not *prevent* one from affirming the unique explanatory status of the fact that x is F with respect to the fact that x exemplifies F-ness.

What can be said about the sort of explanation relation (E) employs? It is an asymmetric metaphysical dependence relation of a kind with those under discussion in Euthyphro-style debates and certain debates in the philosophy of mind. If we admit the necessary equivalence of a pair of distinct facts, we may ask whether there is a relation of explanation holding between them. In the familiar Platonic discussion, the question was whether what makes something holy is the fact that the gods love it or whether the gods love things because they are holy. A more recent discussion assumes the necessary equivalence of being red and looking red to standard observers under standard conditions and asks whether there are explanatory relations between such facts: Are red things disposed to look red because they are red, or are they red because they are disposed to look red?[14] Explanatory questions naturally arise given the recognition of necessary biconditional connections that hold between contingent propositions and that do not admit of explanation in terms of logic, narrowly conceived. A philosophical behaviorist does not simply assert the existence of necessary connections between facts about pain and facts about dispositions to behave, she takes facts about pain to *reduce* to—to have as their *explanantia—facts* about dispositions to behave. Even if philosophical reductions of properties are thought to state property *identities*, someone who denies reductionism about pain may well wish to affirm the metaphysical dependence of facts about pain upon facts about physical states. Kim (1993a, pp. 166-7) shows that the affirmation of strong supervenience is insufficient for this purpose, as strong supervenience does not insure asymmetric dependence.[15]

Note that (E) leaves open the question of the direction of the explanation relation: philosophers who appeal to properties to solve the problem of the One and the Many will insist that the fact that the lemon exemplifies tartness is explanatorily prior; philosophers inclined toward deflationism about exemplification will insist that the explanatory priority lies with the fact that the lemon is tart.

To keep things simple, I leave (E) as it is, while noting possible modifications.

[13] The notion of a fact employed here and throughout is nothing more than that of a truth. One might reject the notion of facts as non-mereological complexes but admit the existence of truths, *i.e.*, true propositions or contents.

[14] See Wright (1992, pp. 108-141), for discussion of the Euthyphro contrast as it relates to contemporary debates over realism and anti-realism.

[15] Perhaps some philosophers will balk at the use the word 'explains' to express the sort of relation I have in mind, as 'explains' often is used to express a relation between persons and phenomena. If so, I invite them to substitute 'constitutes' or 'metaphysically asymmetrically depends'.

A Challenge from David Lewis

Lewis's theory flouts requirement (E). For, given his theory, facts about the mere existence of *possibilia*, together with set-theoretical facts, fully account for all the facts, with respect to the *possibilia* and properties, about which of the former exemplify which of the latter. No contribution is made by the qualitative characters of *possibilia*. Lewis might reply that, on his theory, facts about the qualitative characters of members of a property will determine whether, for example, the property is the property of redness, squareness, quarkhood. Thus, a property Q is the property of quarkhood, if it is, presumably, *because* its members are the quarks. But this at most gives the result that, where q^* is a quark distinct from q, the fact that q^* is a quark is no more and no less explanatorily relevant to the fact that q exemplifies quarkhood than the fact that q is a quark. The quarkiness of each and every quark, as well as the non-quarkiness of each and every non-quark, is equally relevant to the identity of quarkhood. Lewis's theory thus prevents its informed advocate from according q's quarkiness a special explanatory role, for given the theory, q's quarkiness could have an explanatory role only if q^*'s quarkiness had no less an explanatory role.

Let me explain this reasoning more formally. For Lewis, the fact that q exemplifies quarkhood, has as its *analysans* the fact expressed by (19):

(19) $q \in$ the set of quarks.

Given a Russellian interpretation of 'the set of quarks', this same fact can be expressed as follows:

(20) There is a unique set S such that for all x, $x \in S$ iff x is a quark, and $q \in S$.

For Lewis, I take it, (the fact expressed by) (20) is the *analysans* of the fact that q exemplifies quarkhood.[16] Now suppose that the fact that q is a quark has an explanatory bearing on the fact that q exemplifies quarkiness. How could this be, given Lewis's theory? (20) clearly entails that q is a quark, but the entailment runs in both directions, and considerations of entailment alone indicate neither fact as a partial *explanans* of the other. But perhaps there is an explanatory chain running from q's being a quark through (20) to q's exemplifying quarkhood. If q's being a quark is a partial *explanans* of (20) and (20) is the *analysans* of the fact that q exemplifies quarkhood, then q's being a quark would qualify as explanatorily relevant to q's exemplification of quarkhood.

(20) is a general fact and might be thought to be explained by its sole instance. I use 'X' as a name for the set that fulfills the conditions (20) specifies:

(21) For all x, $x \in X$ iff x is a quark, and $q \in X$.

---

[16] When I speak of (20) being the *analysans* of a fact, I mean that *the fact expressed by the sentence flanking the expression '(20)'* is the *analysans* of the fact in question. (To be precise, we would have to say that any fact that is expressed by an instance of the linguistic schema flanking '(20)' is the *analysans* of the fact named by the relevant instance of the schema 'the fact that q is in the set of quarks'.) The use of numerals or acronyms in philosophy often introduces ambiguity: Does the numeral pick out the sentence flanking it or does it pick out what the sentence expresses? Throughout this essay, I leave it to context to disambiguate.

And now the thought might be that q's being a quark helps to explain the general fact that for all x, $x \in X$ iff x is a quark, *i.e.*, the fact that X is the property of quarkhood. The latter fact is presumably explained by the conjunction of all facts of the form <Either $x \in X$ and x is a quark, or $x \in X$ and x is not a quark>, together perhaps with a "full inventory" fact which states "*this* is all the things there are."[17] Each of these disjunctive facts, in turn, is presumably explained by its true disjunct, which is either a fact of the form <$x \in X$ and x is a quark> or one of the form <$x \in X$ and x is not a quark>. Finally, these conjunctive facts are explained jointly by their conjuncts. So, since q is a quark, the fact that q is a quark will enter into the explanation of the fact that q exemplifies quarkhood.

The problem, again, is that even if this way of accommodating the explanatory relevance of q's being a quark to q's exemplification of quarkhood succeeds, it does not accord a unique such status to q's quarkiness: q^*'s quarkiness and my cat's nonquarkiness play no less an explanatory role.

Might counterfactuals help? For Lewis, (22) will be true while (23) false.

(22) If my lemon had not been tart, it would not have been a member of {z:z is tart}.

(23) If your lemon had not been tart, my lemon would not have been a member of {z:z is tart}.

Why isn't this sufficient for the claim that my lemon's being tart is uniquely explanatorily relevant to my lemon's exemplifying tartness?[18] This question has already been answered, implicitly, in our earlier observation that the entailment between x's being F and x's exemplifying F-ness runs in both directions. The problem is that the explanation relation at issue in (E) is asymmetric. Yet if the truth of (22) and the falsity of (23) are jointly sufficient for the explanatory dependence of exemplifying tartness on being tart, then the truth of (24) and the falsity of (25) are jointly sufficient for the converse dependence:

(24) If my lemon had not been a member of {z:z is tart}, it would not have been tart.

(25) If your lemon had not been a member of {z:z is tart}, my lemon would not have been tart.

which is impossible given the asymmetry of the explanatory dependence.

Granted, counterfactual dependence is insufficient for explanatory dependence, is it at least necessary? Does the falsity of (23) at least insure that *your* lemon's being tart is *not* explanatorily relevant to my lemon's exemplifying tartness, given Lewis's theory? We can say this, but only at a high price. We have seen in the above discussion that the most promising strategy, indeed I think the only strategy, available to Lewis for securing the explanatory relevance of the fact that x is F to the fact that x exemplifies F-ness is to cite the fact that x is F as explanatorily relevant to the fact

---

[17] Ernest Sosa suggested to me the apt expression 'full inventory fact'.
[18] I thank a referee for raising this question.

that a certain set is the property of *F*-ness, *i.e.*, *is* the set of *F*s. But this does not distinguish *x* from any other *F*, or for from any non-*F*. The cost of accommodating the explanatory relevance of *x*'s being *F* to *x*'s exemplifying *F*-ness, under Lewis's theory, is flouting (E). If Lewis is right about exemplification, then either the tartness of my lemon is explanatorily irrelevant to its exemplifying tartness or else the tartness of my lemon is no more relevant than the tartness of *your* lemon.

Nor can Lewis satisfy the demands of (E) by saying that the fact that an object is *F is one and the same as* the fact that the object is a member of the set of *F*s, which, in turn, is one and the same as the fact that the object exemplifies *F*-ness. First, to say *that* is to commit oneself to identifying facts about the intrinsic character of an object—*e.g.*, its being a quark[19]—with facts about its external relations to other things—its being a member of a certain set.[20] Second, explanation relations are asymmetric. If the fact that *q* is a quark is identical with the fact that *q* exemplifies quarkhood, then if the former fact explains the latter, Leibniz's Law assures us that the latter explains the former, contrary to the asymmetry requirement. Third, identification of facts of the form <*x* exemplifies *F*-ness> with their cousins of the form <*x* is *F*> creates problems for explaining the logical differences between the following sorts of arguments:

> Kemp exemplifies all the good qualities Dole exemplifies.
> Sagacity is a good quality.
> Dole exemplifies sagacity.
> ∴ Kemp exemplifies sagacity.

> Kemp exemplifies all the good qualities Dole exemplifies.
> Sagacity is a good quality.
> Dole is sagacious.
> ∴ Kemp is sagacious.

The legitimacy of former argument, unlike that of the latter, is guaranteed simply by virtue of logical form.[21]

Similar considerations cast doubt upon Lewis's theory of truth. Analogous to Requirement (E), we have Requirement (T) imposed on theories of truth:

> (T)   Where, at world *W*, <*p*> is true, an adequate theory of propositional truth ought to be compatible the claim that world *W* has the following

---

[19] A word on terminology. I use locutions of the form 'fact about the intrinsic character of *x*' exclusively to denote intrinsic, non-relational facts about objects—the fact that object *x* is red, for example. So relational facts such as the fact that the property *redness* is exemplified by object *x* are not counted as facts about the intrinsic character of objects. I believe this usage comports with Lewis's.

[20] Externality of relations is discussed in the Section II of this essay. Given Lewis's definition of 'external relation', set membership is external.

[21] One might ask: where *x* is *F*, doesn't *x* have a unique explanatory status in respect of its exemplifying *F*-ness in the sense that *x*'s being in the set of *F*s is determined only by whether *x* is in the set, not whether anything else is? I reply: Even supposing the *individual x* has the specified unique explanatory role, (E) requires that *the fact* that *x* is *F* have such a role.

> unique explanatory status in respect of the fact that, at W, $<p>$ is true: W is the only world such that the fact that, at it, p, is explanatorily relevant to the fact that, at W, $<p>$ is true.[22]

Given (T), if $<$Ocean water is salty$>$ is true at world W, the fact that, at W, ocean water is salty is explanatorily relevant to the fact that, at W, $<$Ocean water is salty$>$ is true, whereas the fact that, at W^* ($\neq W$), ocean water is salty is not. Lewis's account fails by (T). If the $<$Ocean water is salty$>$ is the set of worlds in which ocean water is salty, and if the truth of a proposition at a world consists in the world's membership in the proposition, the fact that, at W, ocean water is salty, if explanatorily relevant at all, is not uniquely explanatorily relevant to the fact that, at W, $<$Ocean water is salty$>$ is true. Explanatory contribution would be made from each fact of the form $<$At W^*, ocean water is salty$>$.

Deflationist Platonism, by contrast, treats the explanatory connections between qualitative character and exemplification of properties and between qualitative character and truth of propositions as constitutive, respectively, of exemplification and truth—thus its deflationary character. Under this view, snow's being white fully accounts for snow's exemplifying whiteness, and the ocean water's being salty fully accounts for the truth of proposition that ocean water is salty. Thus, Requirements (E) and (T) are trivially met. Part of the essential justification for Deflationist Platonism is the conviction that (E) and (T) are proper requirements on theories of exemplification and truth, together with the recognition that analyses of exemplification and truth fail by (E) and (T).

Note also that there is a weaker theory of exemplification (truth)—the weaker Weak Deflationist theory discussed in previous chapters—which is in fact consistent with Lewis's own theory of exemplification (truth), also fares well by requirement (E) ((T)). The theory is formulated as follows:

> For all properties P, P is necessarily equivalent to the property with respect to P of exemplifying it.
>
> (For all propositions P, P is necessarily equivalent to the proposition with respect to P that it is true.)

This theory, when conjoined with Lewis's theory of properties (propositions), leads naturally (although, as we will see shortly, not with necessity) to Lewis's theory of exemplification (truth). Nonetheless, a Platonist may affirm the above thesis as a theory of exemplification, in which case we obtain a view that combines deflationism about exemplification (truth) with Platonism about properties (propositions). The view obtained is weaker than Deflationist Platonism, however, insofar as it does not explicitly require explanatory relations between properties and their exemplification correlates (propositions and their truth-ascribing correlates). Nonetheless, such a view does not flout (E) ((T)), since the view is compatible with claims of such explanatory relations.

---

[22] Here, as in (E), the locution 'the fact that at...p' is to be read in Russellian fashion as 'the fact with respect to...that at it, p'.

We should therefore reject concrete modal realist theories of exemplification and truth, but for reasons independent of concrete modal realism's ontological profligacy or its plausibility as an account of modality. Our case hinges on Requirements (E) and (T), which ought to count as common ground in disputes about exemplification and truth. It is the concrete modal realist's analysis of the exemplification of properties (truth of propositions) in terms of membership in sets that leads to the violation of the requirement. *That* the chosen sets are sets of (or set-theoretical constructions from) *possibilia* is immaterial. We see, then, that Requirements (E) and (T), for all their intuitive appeal and seeming innocence, are surprisingly powerful in their consequences. If what (E) presupposes to be true of properties is true of them, the exemplification of a property by an object does not consist in the object's being a member of the property. If what (T) presupposes to be true of propositions is true of them, the truth of a proposition at a world does not consist in the world's being a member of the proposition. We cannot infer from these findings, without additional argument, that Lewis is wrong about the nature of properties and propositions. For all we have said, properties might be sets of *possibilia*, propositions sets of worlds. We *can* infer, however, that even if Lewis is right about the nature of properties and propositions, his theories of exemplification and truth are unacceptable, and so not genuine analyses.

This answers the first part of the challenge to Platonism.

II. THE SECOND PART OF THE CHALLENGE

In his discussion of ersatz modal realism, Lewis (1986, pp. 174-90) considers what he calls "magical ersatzism," a view which invokes abstract, simple entities—among them entities standardly called "properties" or "propositions" or "states of affairs", *etc.*—which are held to represent concrete things truly or falsely, consistently or inconsistently. A possible world, according to such theorists, is a maximal consistent entity of this sort (or perhaps a complex entity built from them). To focus our discussion, let us focus on the case of properties. What goes for properties goes for propositions (and states of affairs if they are different from propositions). The dilemma Lewis presents for magical ersatzism is, in essence, a dilemma for Platonism. The magic in magical ersatzism is Platonist magic.

To prevent our familiarity with talk of "property", "proposition", *etc.*, from compromising our objectivity, Lewis resolves to call the magician's entities *elements* (Lewis 1986, 174). Here, then, is how the magical account goes. Parts of the concrete world *select* some elements and not others. Thus, if snow is white, a certain element is selected by snow, *whiteness*. The entirety of concrete existence selects a maximal element, a *way things might have been*.

Selection, for the magician, is primitive. But even primitives can be illuminated through classification. So Lewis asks: What sort of relation is selection, under the magical theory? Is it an internal or an external relation?

> ...I want to know more about the relation whereby the concrete world 'selects'
> some elements, maximal and otherwise. I ask: is selection an internal relation or

an external relation? That is: is it determined by the two intrinsic natures of its two *relata*? Or is it determined not by the intrinsic natures of the *relata* taken separately, but only by the intrinsic nature of the composite of both of them: element plus concrete world? (1986, p. 176)

Now for the dilemma: either the magician's selection relation is internal or external; if it is internal, we have no inkling of what it is; if it is external, we are saddled with unintelligible necessary connections; neither consequence is acceptable; so we should not accept magical ersatzism. This dilemma translates into a dilemma for Platonism: either the Platonist's selection relation is internal or external; neither alternative is acceptable; so we should give up Platonism.[23] This is the second part of the challenge to Platonism.

Internal relations, according to Lewis, do not differ between duplicates. Thus, a relation R-ing is internal iff where x and w are duplicates and y and z are duplicates, then xRy iff wRz (Lewis 1986, 62). A relation R-ing is external iff (i) R-ing is not internal and (ii) where $x+y$ is a duplicate of $w+z$, then xRy iff wRz. Spatial relations are paradigm external relations, relations of similarity in color and similarity in shape paradigm internal relations. Some relations fall into neither category, e.g., *being married to the same person*.

Is selection internal, external or neither? Borrowing and expanding terminology from van Inwagen (1986, p. 208), the claim that selection is internal is a conjunction of two claims, that it is *range-internal* and that it is *domain-internal*. Selection is range-internal iff where w and z are duplicates, then for any x, x selects w iff x selects z; it is domain-internal iff where x and y are duplicates, then for any z, x selects z iff y selects z. Selection is clearly domain-internal. But is it range-internal? Answering this question requires commitment on the question of whether elements have duplicates other than themselves. If they do, it seems all elements must be pairwise duplicates, in which case selection is *not* range-internal. If they don't, selection is both domain- and range-internal, and so an internal relation. Platonism, as I have formulated it, is non-committal on the issue of whether elements have duplicates other than themselves. But since, as Lewis points out, the prospects are dim for citing, or even imagining the existence of, intrinsic features sufficient to distinguish any two elements, I shall simply concede the first horn of Lewis's dilemma: Platonist selection is not internal.[24]

---

[23] We focus throughout on intrinsic properties (elements). If selection of intrinsic Platonist properties is unintelligible, there is little to save Platonism. Lewis focuses on intrinsic elements, I believe, because he is principally concerned with the case in which the entire concrete world selects an element, a way things could have been, and ways things could have been are intrinsic elements.

[24] I have reservations about this concession. Colors, it seems, are bound together by similarity relations. Redness and greenness share an intrinsic feature that triangularity and trilaterality lack. Moreover, among the colors, there are relations of similarity and dissimilarity: scarlet is more similar to maroon than to indigo. These similarities and dissimilarities, it seems, are due to the intrinsic features of the properties involved. These reflections encourage the thought that intrinsic differences can be found to distinguish at least some properties from one

Is Platonist selection external? We work with the assumption that all elements are duplicates. Consider two duplicate apples, A_1 and A_2, both bright red. Is A_1+redness is a duplicate of A_2+greenness? Where we are concerned with "mixed" sums, *i.e.*, sums of concrete and abstract objects, we might think that if—and only if—the parts of two sums can be put in one-one correspondence under the relation *being a duplicate of*, the sums must themselves be duplicates. Call this principle the "mixed sum duplication principle." Sums of concrete objects might not be duplicates despite fulfilling these conditions. Where apples $A_1,..., A_4$ are duplicates, A_1+A_2 might differ intrinsically from A_3+A_4, insofar as A_1+A_2 differs in its spatial properties from A_3+A_4. If we distinguished mixed sums from sums of concreta in accord with the mixed sum duplication principle, Platonist selection would clearly be non-external. For, given the fact that A_1 and A_2 are duplicates, together with the fact that redness and greenness are duplicates, the principle about mixed sums would dictate that A_1+redness and A_2+greenness are duplicates, despite the fact that A1 selects redness while A_2 does not select greenness. But note that the sum A_1+redness differs from the sum A_2+greenness insofar as it is a sum of two entities one of which selects the other.[25] *If* this difference is a difference in intrinsic character, we might block the conclusion that A_1+redness and A_2+greenness are duplicates. We might thereby save the major premise of Lewis's dilemma, that selection is either internal or external, for selection would clearly be external if it is not internal. I shall assume for the sake of argument that the mixed sum duplication principle is false.

So all hinges on the external horn of the dilemma. Suppose, then, that Platonist selection is external. Lewis claims that this supposition forces the Platonist to accept unpalatable necessary connections. In examining his argument, let us bear in mind three types of necessary connection commonly thought mysterious, the third of which is the focus of Lewis's attack on Platonism:

Type 1 Necessary connections between facts about a thing's intrinsic characters.

Examples: connections deriving from incompatibility of determinates of the same determinable, *e.g.*, if something is round, it is not square; connections between determinables, *e.g.*, if something is colored, it is extended.

Type 2 Necessary connections inexplicable by standard logic between facts about the existence of a thing and facts about its *external* relations to distinct things

Example: membership connections, *e.g.*, David Lewis exists iff he is a member of his singleton.

Type 3 Necessary connections inexplicable by standard logic between facts about the *intrinsic character* of a thing and facts about its *external* relations to distinct things.

Example: Platonist selection connections, *e.g.*, snow selects the Platonic simple, *whiteness*, iff snow is white.

---

another. But there is ample room for skepticism about the claim that, for any two properties, there are intrinsic features in which they differ.

[25] I thank Ernest Sosa for emphasizing to me the importance of this difference.

It is implausible to reject all necessary connections of the first two kinds. The exclusionary relations between the colors and set membership perhaps elude our satisfactory understanding, but are seemingly undeniable nevertheless. Is there anything more objectionable about Type 3 connections? In particular, is there any significant difference in mysteriousness between Type 2 and Type 3 connections? If not, then since we are committed to recognizing Type 2 connections by our acceptance of set theory, we should not count Type 3 connections unacceptable *tout court*. This point is made by Peter van Inwagen (1986) in his *tu quoque* argument against Lewis. Van Inwagen argues that a parallel dilemma confronts Lewis by virtue of his acceptance of set theory. Membership is either internal or external. If internal, we have no idea of the intrinsic features of the *relata* by virtue of which one is a member of the other. If external, we obtain problematic necessary connections.

We might still reject Platonist Type 3 connections if we found that their acceptance, unlike the acceptance of connections supporting set theory, to be philosophically useless. But appeal to Platonist selection is not useless. We may invoke selection relations to explain what it is for word and mental state tokens to be *true of* or *false of* objects, as well as what it is for sentence and mental state tokens to be true or false:

> A word or mental state token is true of an object iff it expresses a property that is selected by the object, and false of an object iff it expresses a property whose complement is selected by the object.

> A sentence or mental state token is true iff it expresses a proposition that is selected (by the actual world), and is false iff it expresses a proposition whose negation is selected (by the actual world).

Given the utility of Platonist selection, and given van Inwagen's *tu quoque*, what justifies Lewis in being dead-set against Platonist Type 3 connections?

Lewis (1991) replies that van Inwagen's *tu quoque* is imperfect. Counterpart theoretic concrete modal realism can explain the necessary connections between concrete objects and their singletons; by contrast, the magician cannot explain necessary connections between intrinsic character and selection of elements. Lewis writes:

> Why *must* Possum be a member of one singleton rather than another? Why isn't it contingent which singleton is his?—But to this I have a reply. On my theory of modality the question becomes: why doesn't some other-worldly counterpart of Possum have a singleton which isn't a counterpart of the singleton that Possum actually has? And my answer is: what makes one singleton a counterpart of another exactly is their having counterpart members...
>
> Now, can the defender of abstract possibilities answer me in a parallel way?—No, because the two complaints involve different kinds of necessary connection...The complaint against singletons involves a necessary connection between external relations and the *identity* of the relatum; where the complaint against abstract simple possibilities involves a necessary connection between external relations and the *qualitative character* of the relatum. The method of counterparts does not apply to the latter problem. (1991, pp. 37-8)

According to Lewis, a necessary and sufficient condition for a singleton {z} to be a counterpart of a singleton {x} is that z be a counterpart of x. Lewis's full explanation can then be formulated as follows:

> For any x, y, y is a counterpart of {x} iff there is a z such that y={z} and z is a counterpart of x. Thus, for any x, all counterparts of {x} contain counterparts of x, and all counterparts of x are members of counterparts of {x}. Therefore, for all x, necessarily, $x \in \{x\}$.

If Lewis is right, counterpart theory renders Type 2 necessary connections between things and their singletons anodyne, but nothing can perform this function for necessary connections between intrinsic character and selection of distinct things. Note that in the above passage, Lewis seems to place all Type 3 connections on a par: Type 3 connections are problematic *regardless of the entities connected*; if Platonism *or any other view* requires such connections, it is unacceptable.

Counterpart theory, I submit, is not up to the task Lewis sets for it. Counterpart relations hold in virtue of broad similarity relations. So it seems that the bedrock *explanandum* Lewis proposes for the necessary connections between objects and their singletons is a fact of the form: <For all x, y, y suitably resembles {x} iff there is a z such that y = {z} and z suitably resembles x>. Granted, the kind of broad resemblance relevant to counterpart relations is not limited to resemblance in intrinsic respects, still one wonders why there should be a necessary connection here. Why should counterpart-conferring similarity of singletons track counterpart-conferring similarity of their members? If we could identify objects with their singletons, there would be no mystery. We cannot. (The null set has no members and so cannot be its singleton, since singletons are non-empty. Why, then, should we suppose some objects are their singletons and others are not? Aside from this, it is hard to believe that I am a set.) Nor can we take objects to be parts of their singletons (See Lewis 1991, pp. 43-5). Membership is one thing, parthood another. But if a singleton's member is neither a part of it nor identical to it, why should its counterpart relations be constrained by those of its member? Appeal to causal relations is unpromising. I conclude that Lewis's use of counterpart theory attempts to explain one puzzling set of connections (connections between objects and their singletons) in terms of an equally puzzling set of connections (connections between the counterpart-conferring similarities of objects and their singletons).

Moreover, nothing in Platonism requires overlap in domains of worlds. A Platonist might accept counterpart theory and subscribe to the following constraint on the counterpart-conferring similarities between elements belonging to different worlds: Element F-ness$_W$ of world W has element E of world W* as a counterpart only if E is selected by all and only the Fs in W*. So redness (the actually existing property) has an element E of a non-actual world W* as a counterpart only if E is selected by all and only the red things in W*. (Counterpart-theoretic Platonism does not collapse into counterpart-theoretic concrete modal realism, for it retains its commitment to abstract simple properties.)

Suppose one defends Lewis's account of the necessary connection between things and their singletons by saying "That's the way we talk. The expression 'the singleton containing Possum' evokes a counterpart-determining relation constrained by the requirement that any counterpart of what is denoted by the expression must be a counterpart of what is denoted by 'Possum'." The counterpart-theoretic Platonist may mimic this reply: "The expression 'redness' evokes a counterpart-determining relation constrained by the requirement that any counterpart of what is denoted by the expression must be selected by all and only red things. That's just the way we talk."

On the one hand, then, van Inwagen's *tu quoque* seems to succeed: if Type 3 connections are problematic for the reasons Lewis gives, Lewis's Type 2 connections are problematic as well. On the other hand, if counterpart theory saves Lewis from van Inwagen's criticism, it saves the Platonist from Lewis's.

I now discuss two additional, more directly damaging, *tu quoque* arguments against Lewis. One concerns David Armstrong's theory of universals, an Aristotelian theory of properties, to which Lewis (1984, 1986) expresses attraction. (It is non-Platonist insofar as it represents genuine properties as non-abstract.) Lewis insists that, for a number of philosophical reasons, we must invoke either perfectly natural classes or something to play the role of perfectly natural classes. The class of grue *possibilia*, for example, is unnatural, whereas the class of green *possibilia*, if not perfectly natural, is at least less unnatural than the class of grue *possibilia*, and the class of *possibilia* that are quarks is perhaps perfectly natural. Among the kinds of entities that would play the role of perfectly natural classes Lewis lists *universals*, conceived of as entities that are *fully present* in their instances as non-spatial parts and that exist in a world only if fully present in some part of that world (Lewis 1984, p. 344). (This supposedly qualifies universals as non-abstract.) Although Lewis does not commit himself to universals, he treats their postulation as a live option in metaphysics (Lewis 1984, p. 343; 1986, pp. 64-5). The *tu quoque* is this: if there are universals, they are involved in necessary connections of Type 3; if Lewis's dilemma succeeds, then Lewis, too, then, is attracted to a view that is thick with Type 3 connections.

Why think there would be necessary connections of Type 3 if there were universals? Selection of a universal by an object consists in part in the object's containing it as a non-spatial part. (Non-spatial parthood cannot be the whole of selection, since the mereological sum of the universal of quarkhood and the Taj Mahal is not itself a quark.) Selection of universals must yield instances of the equivalence schema for selection, where the instances of the schema are restricted to predicates expressing universals. For example, the universals theorist must deliver the necessity: for any x, necessarily, x selects quarkhood iff x is a quark. So if the universals theorist's selection relation is external, we have a necessary connection of Type 3. And plainly, it is. For it is either internal or external. Suppose it is internal. Then there must be some intrinsic features of universals relevant to the determination of selection relations, and we have no idea of what these could be.

The universals theorist might reply as follows. "Not all Type 3 necessary connections are problematic; some such connections are acceptable because they involve mereologically overlapping *relata*. Since I claim that selection of universals involves having them as non-spatial parts, the Type 3 necessary connections I admit are not problematic." If this line of response is to succeed, however, the universals theorist must tell us why a thing's having a universal F-ness as a non-spatial part should correlate with its being F and vice versa. Consider the following standard examples illustrating the link between having a certain part and having a certain intrinsic character. A thing's having a red surface area as part insures its being red; a thing's having a part with a mass of 1 kg insures its being at least 1 kg in mass; a thing's having as a part a rigid 5x5x5 hunk of metal insures something about its dimensions. Contrast the case of universals. F-ness itself cannot be counted on to be F, *e.g.*, quarkhood is not a quark. In fact, universals in general lack the sorts of intrinsic features of the concrete objects that instantiate them; they lack mass, size, shape, color. So how can possession of a mass or size universal as a part help to account for a fact about a thing's mass or size? In general, it seems that we understand how possession of a part can affect a thing's intrinsic character in terms of the intrinsic character of the part itself. But we know little, if anything, about the intrinsic characters (if any) distinguishing distinct universals. (If all universals are counted as duplicates of one another, the problem is severe in the extreme.) We are therefore unable to understand why having *being precisely 1 kg in mass* as a part should correlate with a thing's being precisely 1 kg in mass while having *being positively charged* as a part should correlate with something quite different, *viz.* a thing's being positively charged.

The universals theorist might say in reply: "But wait. I said that instantiation of a universal requires possession of it as a non-spatial part, not that it consists in that relation. You cannot therefore demand that I explain how mere possession of a universal as a part should insure something about intrinsic character." I agree. But I emphasize that the invocation of the parthood relation by itself does nothing to assist the universals theorist in explaining the necessary connections between instantiation of universals and intrinsic character. And I am unable to see how whatever filling is supplied for the equation 'For all x, universals U, x instantiates U iff U is a non-spatial part of x &...', will interact with the parthood condition so as to underwrite explanations of the relevant necessary connections.

A second *tu quoque* strikes closest to home, as is brought out by van Inwagen (1986, p. 210) at the end of his article. Set membership is not an internal relation, for duplicates can differ in their membership properties (Lewis 1991, p. 34). It holds, when it does, only in virtue of the mere existence of its *relata*. What determines that Lewis is a member of {Lewis} is the fact that Lewis and {Lewis} exist. So, Lewisian *selection* is an external relation that holds in virtue of the identity of its *relata*. Even if Lewis and Twin Lewis are duplicates and {Lewis}and {Twin Lewis} are duplicates, Lewis+{Lewis} and Twin-Lewis+{Twin-Lewis} may fail to be duplicates, owing to their differing in the property of having two parts one of which is a member of the other. Now since Lewis identifies quarkhood, for example, with the set of possible quarks, as he must if he is to derive the equivalence <For all x, necessarily, x exemplifies quarkhood iff x is a quark>, he is committed to the existence of a necessary connection between things' being quarks and their membership in the set of possible quarks. This is a Type 3 necessary connection, and one for the explanation of which appeal to mereology is out of the question. So if Lewis's dilemma undermines Platonism, a parallel dilemma undermines his own theory.

What is missing from van Inwagen's discussion and needs emphasis is the observation that the admission of Type 3 necessary connections is endemic to property realism as such. Any adequate realist theory of properties must deliver the equivalences of the form 'For all x, necessarily, x exemplifies F-ness iff x is F' in which 'F-ness' names a genuine property. And since the prospects for identifying intrinsic characters of properties sufficient to differentiate any two of them are poor, any such theory seems saddled with Type 3 connections. Thus, Lewis's dilemma does not single out any defect unique to Platonism. If his dilemma succeeds, it succeeds against property realism as such, and so against both the universals theory and Lewis's own concrete modal realist theory.

One might ask whether Lewis can avoid our *tu quoque* arguments by affirming structuralism in set theory.[26] As Lewis sees it, the chief obstacle to reducing set theory to the sound metaphysics of mereology is the mystery surrounding the singleton function (1993, p. 3). The subset relation is readily reduced: one set is a subset of another iff it is a part of it. And membership can be defined in terms of 'singleton': x is a member of set S iff the singleton of x is part of S. Lewis (1991, pp. 46-7) hopes to tame the notion of a singleton by Ramsification. There is not one singleton function but many; every function that satisfies certain formal (structural) conditions *is* a singleton function.[27] Set-theoretical sentences are thus understood to hide a universal form:

For any singleton function s,—s—s—

To complete the reduction of set theory, sentences quantifying over functions are reconstructed as plurally quantified sentences whose variables range over individuals.

---

[26] This question was raised by a referee.

[27] The relevant conditions are specified as follows:

> A *singleton function* is any unary one-one function S such that
> (0) the range of s consists of atoms (called *s-singletons*);
> (1) the domain of s consists of all small fusions of s-singletons together with all things (called *s-individuals*) that have no s-singletons as parts;
> and
> (2) all things are generated from the s-individuals by iterated applications of s and of fusion.

where something is *small* iff its atoms do not correspond one-one with all the atoms (1993, 16). Lewis adds that we may distinguish the correct singleton functions from the rest. A singleton function is correct iff its division between individuals and classes—that is, its division between s-individuals and fusions of s-singletons—agrees with ordinary assumptions about which are the things that are individuals. Lewis calls the latter "unofficial axioms." He explicitly denies that among these axioms are claims about the whereabouts and character of classes (1993, p. 17). For our purposes, we may ignore the distinction between correct and incorrect singleton functions. My subsequent references to singleton functions may be taken as references to correct ones.

Let us see how Lewis's structuralism bears on his property realism. In the paper in which he explicitly endorses structuralism, Lewis's chief concern is the language of mathematics, the sentences of which, after elimination of defined terms and the reconstruction of 'singleton', involve only the vocabularies of logic and mereology. But suppose we add the following items to the language: a name 'Tabby' which picks out an orange cat Tabby, the predicate 'is orange' which is true of the orange things, and finally an incomplete term 'orangeness', short for the open expression 'the entity E such that for all x, x is part of E iff there is some orange y such that $x=s(y)$'. (We will expand definite descriptions in a Russellian fashion.) We will say that an unreconstructed sentence of the language is true iff its set-theoretical reconstruction 'For all s,—s—s—' is true. Consider now the reconstruction of the sentence 'Tabby exemplifies orangeness':

(26) For all s, there is a unique entity E such that for all x, x is part of E iff there is some orange y such that $x=s(y)$, and s(Tabby) is part of E.

(26) is true iff 'Tabby is orange' is true, and necessarily so.

So far so good. But structuralism has broader consequences, which need to be examined. One such consequence is that exemplification is relativized to singleton functions:

(27) For all P, x, and s, x exemplifies P relative to s iff $s(x)$ is part of P.

Presented with (27), one might expect the property variable to be instantiable to familiar property designators of the form 'F-ness'. But this expectation is unfulfilled. Given Lewis's framework, although there are properties, absolutely speaking, none of them is orangeness, for there is no such thing as orangeness *simpliciter*, there is only orangeness relative to s, orangeness relative to s', *etc.*, and many such "orangenesses" are distinct. The reason for this is that the restrictions Lewis provides on singleton functions, as he points out,[28] allow for many different pairings between individuals and singletons and so for many different pairings between individuals and properties. If there is no such thing as orangeness *simpliciter*, it is of course nonsense to ask after its *de re* modal properties. Lewis therefore will have to reject as unintelligible the *de re* modal claim that orangeness is necessarily such that it is exemplified by all and only orange things.

For Lewis, then, there are properties, but none of them is orangeness, squareness, or quarkhood. Yet we thought there were properties, presumably, because we thought that there were such things as orangeness, squareness, and quarkhood, and that their common feature was their status as attributables, as exemplifiables. The entities Lewis calls properties thus seem not to answer to the intuitions motivating property realism, making it doubtful that they deserve the name.

Of course, Lewis might respond with the addition of substantive requirements on singleton functions, which would jointly guarantee agreement between singleton functions on the identity of orangeness. But these additions would again render Lewis vulnerable to our *tu quoque* arguments, since their combined effect would be

---

[28] See Lewis (1993, p. 17).

to assert the existence of *de re* necessary connections between things intrinsic characters and their exemplification of properties (for Lewis, their membership in sets). Structuralism would give way to substantivism.

Might Lewis remain structuralist and simply reject *de re* necessary connections involving properties? Not if he is to remain a property realist. After all, according to property realism, there *are* such things as properties, and they are genuine entities about which we can ask questions we ask of other sorts of entities: Are they concrete or abstract? Do they depend for their existence on language or thought? Properties, for the property realist, are attributables and exemplifiables, and so she ought to be able to ask after their *de re* necessary connections with the things to which they may be attributed and which may exemplify them. She must ask questions such as:

> Is there a property that is necessarily such that for any x, x exemplifies it iff x is orange?

> Is there a property that is necessarily such that for any x, x exemplifies it iff x is a quark?

If her theory demands that every such question either be answered in the negative or rejected as unintelligible, her theory seems not to qualify as a form of property realism.

For Lewis, then, structuralism is a double-edged sword. Without it, his theory of properties remains realist but vulnerable to our *tu quoque* arguments. With it, he is prevented from admitting the sorts of Type 3 necessary connections essential to property realism.

Necessary connections of Types 1-3 have an air of metaphysical mystery. They resist explanation in terms of the empirical facts supplemented with the facts of logic, narrowly construed. However, in these cases metaphysical mystery is accompanied with epistemic clarity. There can be little doubt that determinates of the same determinable exclude one another; that objects, necessarily, are members of their singletons; that things, necessarily, exemplify whiteness iff they are white. Whatever doubt attaches to these claims attaches to them in virtue of their existential presuppositions. Conditionalized reformulations eliminate the doubt that remains: *if* there are determinates and determinables, they necessarily exclude one other; *if* there are singletons, things are necessarily members of their singletons; and *if* there is a property of whiteness, then, necessarily, things exemplify it iff they are white.

That there *are* properties (features, attributes) of things is a Moorean fact (if a fact at all). *That* properties are *simples* or *complexes*, that they are *abstract* or *concrete*, that they are or are not *sets*, are not. The claim that, necessarily, snow is white iff snow exemplifies whiteness is utterly obvious to all who have the relevant concepts.[29] This is why we should demand a theory of properties to deliver this necessity. In defense of the property realist's selection relation, I claim that if the price of epistemic and

---

[29] Again, barring doubts about the existence of whiteness. Conditionalization may be required to insure obviousness.

conceptual clarity about exemplification is to embrace a metaphysical mystery, a mystery similar to others with which we are already saddled for other mandatory reasons, then the price is not too high. The price of accepting the necessity of the equivalence <Snow exemplifies whiteness iff snow is white> is therefore one we can and should pay. Similar considerations apply in the case of realism about propositions, which brings with it commitments to the necessity of equivalences of the form <<*p*> is true iff *p*>.

Perhaps I underestimate the cost and overestimate the benefit of realism about properties and propositions. My principal aim in this chapter, however, has been only to defend Platonism against a concrete modal realist challenge. If my arguments have been sound, we may draw the following consequences. First, Deflationist Platonism, unlike the concrete modal realist theory, yields the exemplification equivalences while satisfying an adequacy requirement for theories of exemplification, Requirement (E). *Mutatis mutandis* for Deflationist Platonism's theory of truth and Requirement (T). Second, Deflationist Platonism, like all theories presupposing property realism, including the concrete modal realist theory, is committed to necessary connections between intrinsic character and exemplification of properties. So if commitment to such connections is a defect, it is a defect of property realism *simpliciter*. *Mutatis mutandis* for the case of propositions. In sum: the challenge to Platonism fails. In fact, we can say this: if property realism is defensible, which I have argued with modest results in Chapter 1, then Weak Deflationism, coupled with Platonism, is to be preferred to its competitor concrete modal realist analyses. It satisfies (E) and (T).

CHAPTER 5
Truthmaking

The "truthmaker" tradition in ontology has taken its lead from the assumption that the fundamental categories of reality are to be identified in terms of kinds of contribution entities may make toward the *grounding* of truths, toward *truthmaking*. Accordingly, the truthmaker theorist identifies candidate categories of reality, *e.g., particular, universal, trope, event*, and from among these, she counts the ones she believes nonempty *categories*. Categorial monists and pluralists disagree on the number of categories, realists and nominalists on whether the candidate category *universal* is a category. The truthmaker *project*, let us say, is the project of determining which of the candidate categories are categories. D.M. Armstrong is perhaps the project's best-known advocate:

> Why do we need to recognize states of affairs?...The answer appears by considering the following point. If a is F, then it is entailed that a exists and that the universal F exists. However, a could exist, and F could exist, and yet it fail to be the case that a is F...It is no good simply adding the fundamental tie or nexus of instantiation to the sum of a and F. The existence of a, of instantiation, and of F, does not amount to a's being F. The something more must be a's being F—and this is a state of affairs.
>
> This argument rests upon a general principle, which, following C.B. Martin, I call the truth-maker principle. According to this principle, for every contingent truth...there must be something in the world that makes it true. (Armstrong 1993, p. 88)

Other recent advocates of the truthmaker project include Bigelow (1988), Fox (1987), Mulligan, Simons, and Smith (1984), Hochberg (1978), Mellor (1991), and Restall (1996).

This chapter will address two questions about the truthmaker project:

> (Question 1) Does pursuit of the project require acceptance of a correspondence theory of truth rather than a deflationist theory?

(Question 2) Is there good reason to think the project will be fruitful?

In Sections I and II, these questions are answered in the negative. In the section III, I offer some thoughts about how the intuitive dictum 'If something is true, something makes it true' can be reasonably construed so as to express a truth.

I. Question 1: Does Pursuit of the Truthmaker Project Require Acceptance of a Correspondence Theory of Truth Rather than a Deflationist Theory?

We will see that an answer to Question 1 is easily given, once we arrive at an acceptable analysis of truthmaking. The primary burden of this section is sketch such an analysis.

The truthmaker project is aimed at determining, for various truths, the kinds of entities that *make* them true. The relevant truth-bearers here are not sentences, belief states, utterances, *etc.*, but their *contents*, propositions. One might claim that sentences and the rest are made true indirectly, being made true by whatever makes true the propositions they express. To focus on nonpropositional truth-bearers, however, is to miss the point of the truthmaker project. The eyes of the truthmaker theorist are fixed squarely on the world, not on our representations of it. Recall the passage from Armstrong cited earlier: Armstrong searches for an answer to the question 'What must exist in order that a be F?' Meaning and representation relations make no appearance. Reference to *truth* and *truth-bearers* enters only to express the generality of the question asked: If some proposition of the form $<a$ is $F>$ is true, what makes it true? Of course, one might have additional interests that can be schematically described as wanting to know what must exist in order that aRb, that *something* is F, that everything is F. Each such interest is comprehended in the fully general question, 'If a proposition is true, what makes it true?'.

It will be useful to make one substantial assumption concerning propositions: that some of them are Russellian, *i.e.*, that some of them are about objects by virtue of containing them as constituents. Where d_1 and d_2 are rigid names or descriptions and pick out the same object, for any predicate Φ, the Russellian proposition expressed by $\lceil d_1$ is $\Phi \rceil$ = the Russellian proposition expressed by $\lceil d_2$ is $\Phi \rceil$. The truthmaker theorist is interested in the first instance in truths that are about objects independently of how they are described. In what follows, the propositions discussed will be exclusively Russellian.

What is it for an entity to *make true* a truth? Suppose we answer Armstrong's question, 'what must exist for a to be F?' in the way he advises, by saying, 'what must exist is a's being F'. Truthmaking, we might think, is a matter of an entity's existing necessitating a truth. This comports with Fox's (1987, p. 189) Truthmaker Axiom:

(1) If p, some x exists such that x's existing necessitates that p.[1]

---

[1] Here, for ease of exposition, I follow Fox in allowing unrestricted summation of entities; given any entities $X_1,...,X_n$, there is a unique entity Y which has as parts each of the Xs and

Truthmaking

Truthmakers and truths are then paired according to the *pairing principle*: x is a truthmaker for the truth-bearer $<p>$[2] iff x's existing necessitates $<p>$. Taken together, these principles treat *making true* as a broadly logical relation. This is a feature of other accounts of truthmaking found in the literature, in particular Mulligan, Simons, and Smith (1984), Bigelow (1988), and Restall (1996).

Note the absence of the word 'true' and its cognates from (1). We can appreciate the naturalness and propriety of reformulating (1) using 'true' if we turn our attention to the *a priori* necessity of the truth-equivalences of the form $<<p>$ is true iff $p>$.[3] In the presence of these equivalences, (1) is guaranteed to be *a priori* equivalent to (2)

(2) If $<p>$ is true, some x exists such that x's existing necessitates that p

(2) is then naturally generalized to yield (3)

(3) For all P, if P is true, then some x exists such that x's existing necessitates P[4]

Here again invocation of truth enables the expression of generality. One can perhaps achieve the desired generality, however, without invoking truth, by appealing to a relation of material implication between propositions.[5] I abbreviate 'materially implies' by '$\rightarrow$'

(4) For all P, $P \rightarrow$ <Some x exists such that x's existing necessitates P>[6]

Deflationists and correspondence theorists alike may consistently accept (4).[7]

Does Fox's principle, (1), or its generalization, provide the principle the truthmaker theorist needs? Restall (1996) has shown that this account, which he calls the *classical entailment account*, yields disastrous results when conjoined with the plausi-

---

which has as parts no entities that do not overlap any of the Xs. (One could perhaps avoid acceptance of unrestricted summation by making use of plural quantification.) Thus, if the combined existence of entities a, b, and c necessitates that p, we may say that it is the existence of the sum of these entities that necessitates that p.

[2] Recall that I am concerned only with Russellian propositions. Thus, '<Socrates is wise>' as used here should be read as *the proposition with respect to Socrates that he is wise*.

[3] Considerations about the liar-like paradoxes may show that some equivalences of this form are not *a priori* necessary, perhaps not even true. For our purposes, though, we can restrict our attention to the truth-equivalences expressed by sentences of the form '$<<p>$ is true iff $p>$' where the substitution class for 'p' is stipulated not to involve 'true', 'false', 'is true of', 'is false of' or any of their synonyms. *These* truth-equivalences are *a priori* and necessary.

[4] The variable 'P' is an objectual variable taking propositions as its values.

[5] Of course, this relation must not itself be explained in terms of truth. Horwich (1990, p. 23) recognizes such a relation. Alternatively, one might invoke necessary implication (broad logical entailment), where this would not be understood in terms of truth.

[6] The designator '<Some x exists such that x's existing necessitates P>' must be understood as picking out a Russellian proposition, *viz.* the proposition with respect to P that some x exists such that x's existing necessitates *it*.

[7] See chapters 2-3 for a discussion of deflationism about propositional truth. Again, if material implication must be explained in terms of truth, then '$\rightarrow$' must be understood as entailment.

ble-seeming Disjunction Thesis, *viz.* that a disjunction of propositions is made true by an object iff the object makes true at least one of the disjuncts. The argument is as follows. On the classical entailment account, necessary truths are made true by everything. So consider a truth <p v not-p>, with <p> contingent. Given the Disjunction Thesis, every entity makes true <p v not-p>, and so every entity makes true either <p> or <Not-p>. Exactly one of these disjuncts is true. Whichever is true is made true by everything. This gives us *truthmaker monism*: every truth is made true by everything. More than this—although Restall does not bring this out in his article—the account gives us plain falsehoods. My coffee cup is not such that its mere existence broadly entails that snow is white.

Restall recommends abandonment of the classical entailment account in favor of the following *appropriate entailment account*. 's' is used as a variable for truthmakers, '$\models$' as short for 'makes true'.

> A *world* Ω <W, ⊂, $\models$> is made up of a collection, W, of truthmakers, ordered by inclusion. So, if s ⊂ s' then s is a part of s'. A world comes equipped with a map $\models$ from truthmakers to propositions, which satisfies the following.

$s \models A$ & B iff $s \models A$ and $s \models B$
$s \models A$ v B iff $s \models A$ or $s \models B$
For every p, there is an s in W where $s \models p$ or $s \models$ not-p
For no s does $s \models p$ and $s \models$ not-p
If $s \subset s'$ and $s \models A$ then $s' \models A$, too.

If Ω's map $\models$ satisfies these constraints, we can show that $\Omega \models A$ v B iff $\Omega \models A$ or $\Omega \models B$, and similarly for conjunction and negation. (Here '$\Omega \models A$' means 'A is true in Ω'. Restall defines the latter as follows: A is true in Ω iff there is an s in W such that $s \models A$.) The account, as Restall puts it, directs us to "look inside possible worlds to see their fine structure of truthmakers." (Restall, 339). Exploiting this structure, we avoid the result that necessary truths are made true by everything while retaining the Disjunction Thesis. Truthmaker monism is thus rejected, but not at the cost of sacrificing the Disjunction Thesis.

The problem, however, is that insufficient content has been given to '$\models$'. As Restall implicitly acknowledges in his discussion of Bigelow, an adequate model of truthmaking must have the consequence that where s is a truthmaker for A, s's existence classically entails A. Restall's constraints on '$\models$', however, do not collectively impose this requirement. We need only rig '$\models$' differently for different worlds. I use subscripts to mark maps of different worlds. Suppose we have two worlds Ω and Ω' such that

Ω:
a's being $F \models_\Omega$ <The event of a's being F exists>.
a's being $F \models_\Omega$ <a is F>.

Ω':
a's being $F \models_{\Omega'}$<The event of a's being F exists>.
a's being $F \models_{\Omega'}$<Not-(a is F)>.

These suppositions are jointly allowable given the constraints.[8] But they jointly entail that although, in Ω, a's being F makes true $<a$ is $F>$, the existence of a's being F fails to classically entail that a is F. I show this using Restall's definition of classical entailment in terms of truthmaking, adding subscripts: A classically entails B iff, for all worlds Ω, if $\Omega \models A$, then $\Omega \models B$. Both Ω and Ω' contain truthmakers for $<$The event of a's being F exists$>$, and so $\Omega \models$ $<$The event of a's being F exists$>$ and $\Omega' \models$ $<$The event of a's being F exists$>$. Given that the set of truthmakers W_Ω of Ω includes an entity s such that $s \models_\Omega <a$ is $F>$, $\Omega \models <a$ is $F>$. Yet, since the set of truthmakers $W_{\Omega'}$ of Ω' includes an entity s such that $s \models_{\Omega'} <$Not-a is $F>$, it is not the case that $\Omega' \models <a$ is $F>$. Thus, classical entailment fails.

What Restall needs, it seems, is one of two stronger constraints. The first is this:

(5)   For atomic proposition $<Ra_1...a_n>$, if $Ra_1...a_n$, then
a_1's R-ing $a_2...a_n \models <Ra_1...a_n>$, and if not-$Ra_1...a_n$, then
a_1's not R-ing $a_2...a_n \models <$Not-$Ra_1...a_n>$.

(5) may give Restall what he needs, but at a prohibitively high cost. An adequate account of truthmaking should not merely have (5) as a consequence, but should *explain* why (5) holds. The classical entailment account does this: what it is for a's being F to make true is for its existence to classically entail that a is F. But simply to append (5) to one's account is not to offer an explanation.

Alternatively, Restall might add constraint (6):

(6)   For atomic A, $s \models A$ iff s exists in Ω and s's existing classically entails A, and $s \models$ not-A iff s exists in Ω and s's existing classically entails not-A.

Supplemented with (6), Restall s account is equivalent to the following recursive account of truthmaking, which employs classical entailment:

(i)   Where A is atomic or the negation of an atomic, $s \models A$ iff s exists and s's existing classically entails A.

(ii)   Where A is (or is a De Morgan equivalent of) a disjunction of B and C, $s \models A$ iff $s \models B$ or $s \models C$.

(iii)   Where A is (or is a De Morgan equivalent of) a conjunction of B

---

[8] But isn't $<$The event of a's being F exists$>$ really just identical with $<a$ is $F>$? If it were, then Ω' would not be allowable under Restall s constraints. But these propositions really are distinct. The truthmaker project is in the business of finding *entities* to serve as truthmakers, even for the atomic truths, not merely to found truths on atomic truths themselves. One might claim that $<$The event of a's being F exists$>$ ontologically explains $<a$ is $F>$, but to say that must not be to imply that $<a$ is $F>$ is one and the same with that proposition. Such a supposition, I think, is out of the question. One does not have to believe in events in order to believe atomic propositions, *e.g.*, that such and such particle is in such and such location.

Some consequences of the suppositions are as follows: in Ω, a's being F will make true every disjunction of the form $<a$ is F v $p>$; in Ω', it will make true every disjunction of the form $<$Not-$(a$ is $F)$ v $p>$. Similarly, for conjunction; in Ω, a's being F will not make true $<$Not-$(a$ is $F)>$; in Ω', a's being F will not make true $<a$ is $F>$.

(iv) and C, $s \models A$ iff $s \models B$ and $s \models C$.
For every p, there is an s where $s \models p$ or $s \models$ not-p.

The addition of (6), too, yields unwanted results. Presumably, there are necessary atomic truths, *e.g.*, that Socrates is human, that such-and-such piece of clay is a piece of clay, that 7 is a number. Even with the addition of (6), these will come out as made true by everything under Restall's account. Truthmaker monism is avoided, but the suspicion remains that the mere fact that my coffee cup's existing entails that Socrates is human is insufficient for its making that proposition true: the mere existence of my coffee cup seems *irrelevant*—explanatorily, though not in the broad logical sense—to whether Socrates is human.[9]

In fact, the locutions 'makes true' and 'grounds the truth of' are explanatory, at least if understood in their more ordinary uses. I submit that the truthmaker theorist—the ontologist interested in discerning the fundamental categories of reality by reference to contribution to truthmaking—does best to follow ordinary use in this regard. Let me explain. The truthmaker theorist's identification of candidate ontological categories must be conducted in the light of ontological constraints, such as the following:

C1. If two atomic truths have the same predicate (*e.g.*, <Socrates is wise> and <Plato is wise>), their truthmakers must "have something in common."[10]

C2. If two atomic truths have different predicates, their truthmakers must "differ in some way."

C3. If two atomic truths share a subject (*e.g.*, <Socrates is wise> and <Socrates is a philosopher>), their truthmakers must "have something in common."

C4. If two atomic truths differ in a subject, their truthmakers must "differ in some way."

These constraints correspond to natural definitions of some of the principal candidate categories:

D1. A *universal* is an entity that is a constituent of every truthmaker for every truth in some equivalence class of truths under the relation of *having the same predicate*.

---

[9] One might think of adding to Restall's account not (6) but the weaker principle: for all atomic A, $s \models A$ only if s's existence classically entails A, and $s \models$ not-A only if s's existence classically entails not-A. But this prompts the question, 'what in addition to classical entailment is required for s to make true atomic A?' And we would be back to our starting point, in need of an account of *appropriate* entailment.

[10] I allow myself talk of "subjects" and "predicates" of propositions. This talk can be given a clear sense when used in connection with Russellian propositions. A Russellian proposition $<Ra_1,...,a_n>$, has as its subjects $a_1,...,a_n$ and as its predicate R-ing.

(Wisdom would be a universal in virtue of being a constituent of every truthmaker for every truth of the form <x is wise>.)

D2. A *trope* is an entity E such that (i), there is one and only one atomic truth P such that E is a constituent of each of its truth-makers, (ii) E exactly resembles but is distinct from every entity E' that meets condition (i) with respect to an atomic truth P' (≠P) that has the same predicate as P.
(The particular wisdom of Socrates would be a trope in virtue of being a constituent of each truthmaker for <Socrates is wise> and exactly resembling, *e.g.*, the particular wisdom of Plato.)

D3. An *individual* is an entity that neither a universal nor a trope but is a constituent of every truthmaker for every truth in some equivalence class of truths under by the relation of *sharing a subject*.
(Socrates would be an individual in virtue of being neither a universal nor a trope and being a constituent of every truthmaker for every truth of the form <Socrates is F>.)

Now suppose we adopt these definitions but refuse to require an explanatory relation for truthmaking, choosing instead to remain with an account in terms of entailment, be it classical or of Restall's *appropriate* variety. Then we must deny that Socrates is an individual. We must equally deny that is there a universal of *humanity* and that there is a trope of Socrates's individual humanity. We would incur these commitments because we would be forced to admit that each and every existent is a truthmaker for <Socrates is human>, so that some of its truthmakers have neither Socrates, nor humanity, nor Socrates's particular humanity as constituents, *e.g.*, my coffee cup. In general, we would be committed to saying that there are no individuals, that there are no universals expressed by predicates that apply essentially if at all, and that there are no tropes expressed by expressions of the form 'particular F-ness of x' where 'F' applies essentially if at all. This is unacceptable. If there are universals, surely *humanity* and *being an atom* are among them, and if there are tropes, surely my particular humanity and a particle's particular atomicity are among them. Moreover, assuming that snowballs are essentially round, we would have the result there is no universal of *roundness* and no trope of such-and-such snowball's particular roundness.

Note that even if it is claimed that the propositions I have listed, <Socrates is human>, <This snowball is round>, *etc.* are contingent, there will be necessary atomic truths about necessary existents, *e.g.*, <7 is a number>, <Red is a color>.[11]

One might reply that necessary truths lack truthmakers, and that the above ontological constraints should be reformulated to adjust for that fact. But this seems

---

[11] Note also that if <Socrates is human> is contingent, because false in those possible worlds in which Socrates doesn't exit, then the non-explanatory reading of 'E makes true P' still seems to give us the result that there is no universal of humanity. For, Socrates himself would be a truthmaker for <Socrates is human> and Socrates would appear not to have humanity as a con-

ad hoc. Necessary truths are truths. Why shouldn't they, too, require foundation in what exists? Not in contingent existence, but in existence nonetheless.

Alternatively, one might substitute 'some' for 'every' appropriately in the definitions of the categories of universal, *etc*. Thus, one might claim that humanity is a universal insofar as it is a constituent of *some* truthmaker for every truth of the form <*x* is human>. Might that be enough to qualify it as a universal? Perhaps, but my coffee cup, too, meets this condition, and presumably it is not a universal. If we take <7 is a number> as our focal atomic truth, *being a number* will count as a universal, but again, so will my coffee cup.

I conclude that the truthmaker theorist ought to insist on an explanatory reading of '*E* makes true *P*', viz. *E is such that its mere existence ontologically explains P*. The explanation relation in question here is asymmetric, absolute and objective, and one that holds necessarily between its *relata* if at all. Moreover, if it holds between *E* and *P*, then for any object *O* that contains *E* as an essential part, it holds between *O* and *P*. One might desire further illumination, of course. But the truthmaker theorist may take some comfort in knowing that she is not alone in using such an explanation relation: a similar (if not identical) relation is used by philosophers who maintain that facts about value ontologically derive from natural facts or that facts about numbers derive from facts about sets.

Given this rough analysis of truthmaking, we have our answer to Question 1: pursuit of the truthmaker project is non-committal with respect to debates in the theory of truth. The truthmaker theorist, without inconsistency, can espouse deflationism about truth for propositions (as well as about truth for any other truth-bearers).[12]

II. QUESTION 2: IS THERE GOOD REASON TO THINK THE TRUTHMAKER PROJECT WILL BE FRUITFUL?

I describe one series of beginning steps in the truthmaker project, perhaps one series among others, but a natural one nevertheless. My aim is to defend a negative answer to Question 2 by arguing that we have good reason to doubt the existence of truthmakers.

---

stituent. A bundle theorist might dispute this claim, but it would surprising to find that the bundle theory is so obviously forced upon truthmaker ontologists.

[12] However, the deflationist truthmaker theorist must take care to refrain from identifying truthmakers by using locutions of the form 'the possible fact that *a* is *F* exists' and 'the possible fact that *a* exemplifies *F*-ness exists', where these are used synonymously with the locutions 'the possible fact that a is F obtains' and 'the possible fact that a exemplifies F-ness obtains'. In other words, she must use 'exists' to express genuine *existence* rather than *obtaining*. To violate this precept is to invoke a truth-like notion, obtaining, in explaining truth-free facts, and more generally to explain a truth by reference to the fact of its being true. To be a deflationist about truth for propositions, however, is precisely to explain the fact of a truth's being true by reference to that very truth. For the deflationist, the fact that snow is white comes first in the order of explanation, and the fact that <Snow is white> is true is explained in terms of it.

Truthmaking 95

How might the truthmaker principle, (7), for atomics,

(7)   If p, there is an x such that x's existing *ontologically explains* <p>

be used to answer the question 'Which candidate categories are categories?'? The truthmaker theorist works with *schemata* for atomic truths. By using schemata, she secures the generality of her findings. She wants her findings to be independent of the facts about the identity of the atomic truths, the facts about whether, for example, the atomic truths concern micro-particles, sense-data, or familiar medium sized objects. The truthmaker project is aimed at determining what *kinds* of things there are, not what particular things there are.

Among the atomic truths, whatever they should turn out to be, there will be monadic truths that are oriented toward the present[13] and involve different subjects but the same predicate. There will also be monadic truths that are oriented toward the present and involve the same subject but different predicates. To save words, I will use the label 'atomic' in what follows only for atomic truths that are oriented toward the present.

The truthmaker theorist may therefore begin her project with simple schemata for atomic truths and for what Fox calls *minimal* truthmakers (truthmakers for a truth A none of the proper parts of which are truthmakers for A (Fox, p. 190)). (I use brackets as summing devices, so that '[x, y, z]' will abbreviate 'the sum of x, y, and z'.)

(8) a is F [...]
        b is F [...]
        b is G [...]

Our theorist asks herself what should replace the dots. Her answer will be guided by a set of appropriate ontological constraints, some of which we have already discussed, *e.g.*: C1-C3. Not to decide in advance for one ontology over another, the language of "having something in common" and "differing in some way" should not be construed as synonymous, respectively, with "sharing a constituent" and "differing in a constituent."[14][15]

Suppose, then, our theorist gives the answer:

---

[13] A truth is oriented toward the present, roughly, if it is solely about what is going on at the present time. One might try to analyze this notion in terms of entailment of contingent truths about the past or future, but one soon encounters difficulties: take a true proposition <p>; <p> entails <In the past <p> was going to be true>; does this disqualify <p> from being oriented toward the present? Presumably not. I leave the notion of "oriented toward the present" intuitive.

[14] Here and throughout I use 'constituent' in a broad sense, so that one is not forbidden by considerations of meaning alone from saying "X is a constituent of Y, although X is not a spatial part of Y."

[15] My rough sketch of the truthmaker theorist's first steps has been influenced by the work of Edwin Allaire (1976). My sketch, however, differs in an important way from his. He imposes a further constraint on the truthmaker project: the entries in the brackets cannot be of a type with what is written to their left. This constraint seems motivated by a concern that

(9) a is F [a, F-ness]
      b is F [b, F-ness]
      b is G [b, G-ness]

Without judging its adequacy, we may say that this answer, by virtue of the reappearance of 'F-ness' in the brackets of the second line, commits our theorist to recognizing a category of *universals*, entities that are constituents of every truthmaker for every atomic truth in an equivalence class of truths under the relation of *having the same predicate*.[16]

We have already defined candidate categories of *individual* and *trope*. A further important candidate category is that of *event*. Let us say that to be a *basic event* is to be an entity that is (i) a truthmaker of an atomic proposition and (ii) not a proper sum;[17] and to be an *event* is to be a sum (proper or improper) of basic events.

From the truthmaker theorist's schemata, we can "read off" the categories she posits. Thus, according to the ontological schema below on the left, there are events, and according to one on the right there are individuals and tropes:[18]

(10) a is F [a's being F]   (11) a is F [a, a's particular F-ness]
      b is F [b's being F] b is F [b, b's particular F-ness]
      b is G [b's being G] b is G [b, b's particular G-ness][19]

---

statements of the form 'what makes it true that a is F is a's being F' are trivial. But if we understand 'makes true' to express an explanatory relation that holds of a pair $(x, <p>)$ only if x's mere existing ontologically explains $<p>$, these statements are significant.

[16] We can infer this general commitment from the few schematic entries in brackets because the truthmaker theorist's interests are perfectly general. The only relations she takes note of between the occurrences of schematic letters are sameness/difference of logical type (eligibility for replacement by name or predicate) and sameness/difference of sign type within a logical type ('a' vs. 'b'). So, if 'c is F' were added to (10), our truthmaker theorist would be obliged to write in the brackets to the right '[c, F-ness]'.

[17] An entity E is a proper sum iff there are entities $E_1, ..., E_n$ such that (i) E is distinct from each of the E_is; and (2) E is the sum of the E_is. Every entity is of course a sum, since every entity is the sum of itself with itself. But (arguably) not every entity is a proper sum.

[18] Since commitment to categories is "read off" the entries in brackets, the theorist who asks herself what to write in brackets must have some conception of the schemata 'a', 'F-ness', "a's being F" and "a's particular F-ness." A truthmaker theorist might simply say that she understands these schemata in an intuitive way just insofar as she understands their instances. She knows the meaning of 'Bill Clinton', 'Friendliness', 'Bill Clinton's being friendly', and (perhaps?) 'Bill Clinton's particular friendliness'. If the truthmaker theorist wished to avoid schemata, she could simply ask herself: "Suppose Bill and Hillary Clinton are friendly, but Scrooge isn't. What entities must exist to account for the fact that Bill Clinton is friendly? Bill Clinton alone is not enough. Friendliness alone is not enough..." The advantage of using schemata, again, is that it enables the theorist to achieve generality.

[19] Once some categories are recognized, new schemata may be constructed. Thus, if universals are recognized, a theorist may be concerned with the additional schemata, 'F-ness is G' and 'F-ness is H', where 'F-ness' is to be replaced by a proper name of a universal. To distinguish varieties of particularity, our theorist might wish to introduce derived categories, *e.g.*,

Our simple description of the first steps in the truthmaker project exposes its fundamental challenge, *viz.* the Bradley problem. Bradley's problem is this: a contingent atomic truth <*a* is *F*> is not entailed, and so *a fortiori* not ontologically explained,[20] by the existence of *a*, nor the combined existence of *a* and *F*-ness, nor that of these together with the dyadic exemplification relation, nor again that of *these* together with any number of higher-order exemplification relations. Bradley's problem shows that we cannot build truthmakers without *events*. Sum as many individuals, universals, tropes, etc., as you like, and you will not have a truthmaker. The recognition of events alone opens the door for ontological debate about further categories. The realist about universals may employ what Bigelow (1987) calls "Robinson's Merger," a strategy which introduces universals as constituents of events—Bigelow uses the term 'property-instance' (1988, p. 151))—as a way of accounting for the commonalty in truthmakers of truths having the same predicate.[21] The nominalist may employ an analogous strategy to introduce tropes, claiming that an event of *a*'s being *F* has as a constituent the trope of *a*'s particular *F*-ness.

Let us look take a closer look at the candidate category of *event*. The term 'event' has a common use that is not obviously associated with truthmaking. A possible connection emerges, however, if we abstract from ordinary distinctions between "events," "states," and "processes." Jaegwon Kim (1976) proposes the following "existence condition" for events:

(12)   Event [x, P, t] exists just in case substance x has property P at time t. (1976, p. 35)

(12) is intended to express a necessary truth. Given the *a priori* necessity of equivalences of the form <x exemplifies F-ness at t iff x is F at t>, (12) entails the instances of the schema

(13)   Event [x, F-ness, t] exists just in case substance x is F at time t

Since we are concerned with truthmakers of truths oriented toward the present, we may work with the simpler

(14)   Event [x, F-ness] exists just in case substance x is F

---

that of a *narrow individual*, *i.e.*, individual that is not an event. The truthmaker theorist may go on to seek truthmakers for propositions ascribing changes in objects over time. Debates may then ensue over whether concrete particulars *endure* or *perdure* through time, *i.e.*, whether their identity over time is a matter of their being fully present throughout their existence or of their being instead partially present at each moment of their existence through the full presence one of their temporal parts.

[20] The power of Bradley's problem is more easily appreciated in application to accidental predications. For where <*a* is *F*> is an accidental predication, the mere existence of a, F-ness, and the exemplification relations is not even logically sufficient for <*a* is *F*>. Nonetheless, even where <*a* is *F*> is an essential predication, the mere existence of a, F-ness, and the exemplification relations fails to ontologically explain <*a* is *F*>.

[21] Bigelow's discussion, however, is misleading in suggesting that property-instances might be construed as mereological sums of universals and particulars.

(14) assures us that, for any atomic truth <x is F>, there is one and only one event x's being F whose mere existence necessitates and is necessitated by it. Let us say, using a terminology similar to that of Jonathan Bennett (1988), that when atomic proposition P bears this relation to event E, P is E's parent proposition (or parent fact if P is true).[22] The truthmaker theorist might then read (14) in the direction of left to right: <The event of a's being F exists> *ontologically explains* <a is F>.

Supposing there are events, *i.e.*, entities that meet Kim's existence condition, do they form a category? Are they truthmakers? In the interest of clarity, let us use 'event' to pick out entities that meet Kim's existence condition, whether or not they form a category, and use 'C-event' to pick out members of the category of event, if it is a category. If there are C-events, events are among them. So our question is whether events are C-events.

Suppose we have an event of a's being F with parent proposition <a is F>. I will offer an argument that <The event of a's being F exists> is ineligible to explain <a is F>. If the argument succeeds, events are not C-events, for the existence of a C-event would need to explain its parent fact, which it could not do if facts are, so to speak, the explanatory parents of their companion events.

We focus on events that do not have events as proper parts, on what we have called "basic events." Now, if an event exists, so does its subject. Suppose that *Bill's smiling (at t)* is a basic event. If *Bill's smiling* exists, then Bill exists. And this is a matter of necessity, giving us a necessary connection between numerically distinct concrete existences. Perhaps we must learn to live with some unexplained necessary connections between distinct existences. But in the case of Bill and his smiling we feel an impulse to try to account for the necessary connection by reference to a constituency relation. We say: *Bill's smiling* is a *complex* and Bill is one of its proper constituents and the fact that the complex exists is explained by facts about the constituents (including Bill) and their interrelations. (Analogously, if a chair is a complex of atoms, it is plausible to think that the existence of the chair is ontologically explained by facts about the character and arrangement of the constituent atoms. In general, facts about constituents are excellent candidates for explainers of facts about complexes.) In the case of the existence of Bill's smiling, the relevant fact about Bill surely is the fact that he is smiling. To say *that*, however, is to give up thinking of events as C-events.

This argument suggests that we should count events as supervenient entities whose existence is accounted for by their parent facts.[23] Furthermore, although the argument is independent of the dispute over deflationism in the theory of truth, it fits particularly well with deflationism. The truth- and event-free facts determine the facts about the existence and character of events as well as the facts about which propositions are true. The fact that Bill is smiling determines both the fact that the

---

[22] Bennett (1988, p. 126) speaks of event *names* as having parent propositions.

[23] See Lombard (1986, p. 213) for an account of the supervenience of events. Bennett (1988, p. 60) cites Lombard's supervenience thesis as firm ground for believing that the times of events are essential to them.

event of Bill's smiling exists and the fact that the proposition <Bill is smiling> is true.

The truthmaker theorist might reply by saying either that (basic) events are *simple* particulars or that they are *independent complexes* (*i.e.*, complexes the existence of which is not ontologically explained by facts about their constituents). The former position is recognizable as Davidson's and the latter as Armstrong's. Neither of these alternatives is attractive: to accept events as simple particulars is to admit unexplained necessary connections between the existence of non-overlapping entities—Davidson himself in giving the logical form of action sentences freely employs the notion of *being a subject of an event*, but does not give us any metaphysical account of the notion; to accept events as independent complexes is to commit oneself to an obscure constituency relation. The inferential transition from 'event' to 'C-event' may be secured by these responses, but at the likely cost of rendering both terms empty. I do not tout these considerations as conclusive, but I think they show that the truthmaker project is troubled. It would be best, if possible, to explain the truthmaking intuitions without presupposing a positive outcome to the truthmaker project.

III. Truthmaking without the Truthmaker Project

There is an undeniable ring of truth in the dictum 'If something is true, something makes it true'. What accounts for this? It seems the dictum has the following ordinary meaning, which is distinct from the meaning attached to it by truthmaker theorists: "If something is true, something accounts for its truth." Regimenting somewhat, we arrive at the principle

(15)   For all P, if P is true, something accounts for the truth of P.

So understood, the truthmaker dictum expresses an obvious truth about *truth*: facts about the truth of propositions are not explanatorily basic. If circles of explanation are ruled out, (15) will assure us that truth is supervenient, that facts attributing truth to propositions are ultimately explainable in terms of facts *not* attributing truth to propositions. The fact that <<Snow is white> is true> is true is explained ultimately by the truth-free fact that snow is white.

So far, the truthmaker theorist can agree. However, she will insist that the explanatorily more basic facts must in the end be singular existential facts, facts about *what exists*. But we need not follow her down this path. In answer to the question 'What accounts for <p>'s truth, if it is true?', we may simply say: the fact that *p*. So, for instance, if <Phoebe is purring> is true, we agree that there is something that accounts for its truth, *viz.* the fact that Phoebe is purring. The *explanans* here is not the *existence* of the fact that Phoebe is purring, but the fact itself. When pressed with the question 'What is it whose existing explains the fact that *p*?', we might reply that there is no general answer available, but that in many (if not all[24]) cases,

---

[24] It is difficult to think of cases in which a fact seems to admit of ontological explanation by a singular existential proposition. Here is one candidate: Does the mere existence of the sum of myself and my singleton ontologically explain the fact that I am a member of my singleton?

the answer is 'Nothing. The fact in question is not ontologically explained by any singular existential fact.' In so answering, we are not saying that all truth-free facts are ontologically rock bottom. For we may admit that there is some ontological story to be told which will illuminate the facts that jointly explain the fact that Phoebe is purring. Our claim would merely be that there is no singular existential fact that explains this fact about Phoebe.

We will want, furthermore, to say something about what *would* make a proposition true, even if it is not true, even if it could not have been true. We want to say that what would account for the truth of <Squares are circles> would be squares' being circles. Using 'explains' to express a relation of explanation analogous to that holding between analytically equivalent propositions, we might then express the fundamental truth behind the truthmaking dictum as follows:

(16)   For all P, P explains the proposition with respect to P that it is true.

This would make explicit the asymmetry left inchoate in the familiar equivalence schema

(17)   <p> is true iff p

These reflections raise an interesting possibility. It may turn out that, once the truthmaking intuitions are seen in the proper light, deflationism, rather than any substantive correspondence theory, makes the best sense of them.[25] A surprising result!

---

[25] A deflationist might take these intuitions, as recorded in the above schema, as explanatory of truth. A correspondence theorist, by contrast, would be faced with the task of explaining why there should be a necessary connection between facts of these sorts: <<p> corresponds to a worldly entity> and <p>.

CHAPTER 6

The Liar Paradox

How can Weak Deflationism be amended to provide a general account of truth that will avoid liar-like paradoxes? Our challenge is to give a *general* account of truth, not merely an account of truth for propositions not involving truth.[1] Our chief obstacle is the phenomenon of liar-like pathology.

Any theory of truth that treats pathological and non-pathological propositions alike is defective. This is true of Horwich's minimalism,[2] Sosa's finite minimal theory (FMT),[3] the finite theory (FT),[4] and the asymmetric finite theory (AFT).[5] To keep things manageable, let us use as our foil just one theory, (FMT). (Any of the others would do, but (FMT) has a welcoming simplicity.)

(FMT)   For all propositions P, P is necessarily equivalent to Tr(P)[6]

Suppose I am mistaken about the time; I believe it is 2:00 when it is in fact 1:00. Since I have little better to do, I turn my mind to the following (timeless) proposition <The proposition I entertain at 1:00 is not true>. I soon afterward glance at the clock! When I entertained the proposition it *was* 1:00. I turn my mind again to that

---

[1] Rather than reverting to the terminology of 'TRUE' for propositional truth, 'TRUE' for non-propositional truth, and 'true' for the disjunction of the two, I will mostly leave it to context to disambiguate 'true'.
[2] Minimalism, construed in a perfectly general way, is the theory the axioms of which are all and only the propositions of the form <<*p*> is true iff *p*> (Horwich 1990, p. 18).
[3] (FMT) is the thesis that for all propositions P, P is necessarily equivalent to Tr(P). Here 'Tr' is used to denote a propositional function, namely the function that takes an entity E and returns the proposition with respect to E that it is true. See Sosa (1993).
[4] (FT) is just like (FMT) but for its employment of the notion of *material* equivalence rather than *necessary* equivalence.
[5] (AFT) is the thesis that for all propositions P, P explains Tr(P).
[6] 'Tr' denotes the function that for an argument x returns the proposition with respect to x that it is true.

proposition. Is it true or not true? Neither answer can be right, it seems, given (FMT). Suppose <The proposition I entertain at 1:00 is not true> is true. Given (FMT), we have

(1)   <The proposition I entertain at 1:00 is not true> is necessarily equivalent to <<The proposition I entertain at 1:00 is not true> is true>

(1), in conjunction with the unproblematic principle of entailment (which holds for both narrowly and broadly logical entailment):

(PE)   <p> entails <q>, only if, p only if q

yields

(2)   The proposition I entertain at 1:00 is not true iff <The proposition I entertain at 1:00 is not true> is true

(2), together with the fact that the proposition I entertain at 1:00 = <The proposition I entertain at 1:00 is not true>, gives us the paradoxical conclusion

(3)   The proposition I entertain at 1:00 is not true iff the proposition I entertain at 1:00 is true

The guilty party, it seems, is the unrestricted version of (FMT), since the principle of entailment (PE) and the facts of the case seem unproblematic. How, then, to amend (FMT)? To simply specify that the quantifier in (FMT) is to range over a domain consisting of "only those propositions that would not, together with the actual facts, entail 'liar-like paradoxes'" would be *ad hoc*. If our account does not entail the truth-equivalences corresponding to the pathological propositions, some principled story must be told explaining why this is. But in addition it seems we need to be told what it *would be* for particular pathological propositions to be true or false. After all, many pathological propositions are only contingently pathological. Consider <The proposition I entertain at 1:00 is not true> itself. Call it P. There is a (remote) world in which at 1:00 I entertain the proposition <The New York Jets won the Superbowl in 1995> and the New York Jets won the Superbowl in 1995. In this world, P is true. Whether P is pathological or not depends upon the contingent facts about what I entertain at 1:00. In general, no purely *a priori* test can be used to judge pathology. An adequate theory of truth, therefore, ought to give us an explanation, with respect to any proposition, of what it would be for it to be true and of what it would be for it to be false. Even if a proposition is necessarily pathological, we will want to know why it is prevented from having a truth-value, and to know this we will need to know what it would be for it to be true (false).

Furthermore, our account must identify a defect unique to pathological propositions which explains their pathological character. We are familiar enough with the paradigm cases: the liars, the truth-tellers. We know their pathological character has something to do with the fact that they "say directly or indirectly about themselves that they are true, false, not true, or not false". Explaining pathology is part and parcel of solving the "liar paradox".

I submit that the supervenient character of truth is the key to answering the challenge posed by the liar-like pathologies. To claim that truth supervenes is at least to claim, (i), that facts attributing or denying truth (or falsity or any other truth-like properties)[7] are determined by facts that do not, and (ii), that the negations of falsehoods attributing or denying truth are likewise determined by facts that do not. If a pair of contradictories, one attributing truth and the other denying it, are not determined, then neither is true or false. Liars and truth-tellers lack truth-value, since neither they nor their negations are determined by the "truth-free" facts.

These thoughts point us in the direction of accounts of truth and falsity for truth-attributing and denying propositions: roughly, for such a proposition to be *true* is for it to be determined by some "truth-free" fact; for such a proposition to be *false* is for its negation to be so determined; if a truth or falsity-attributing or denying proposition is pathological, neither it nor its negation is determined in the manner required, and so lacks truth-value.

This is only a first stab. The notions of "truth-free propositions" and "truth (falsity)-attributing (denying) propositions" are perhaps clear enough: the truth-free are the propositions that do not involve truth at all, neither propositional truth, sentential truth, *etc.*,[8] the truth-attributing are values of Tr, the truth-denying values of Neg-Tr, the falsity-attributing values of Fls, the falsity-denying values of Neg-Fls. But if ours is to be a perfectly general account of truth, it must apply to *all* propositions involving truth, not merely to those attributing or denying truth or falsity. For example, our account must explain what it is for the truth-equivalence <<Snow is white> is true iff snow is white> to be true, but this proposition involves truth but neither attributes nor denies it.

The parallels between this "first stab" and Kripke's (1975) treatment of the liar are clear. In the final section of this chapter, I will argue that the supervenience intuition provides a sound philosophical basis for Kripke's (1975) account and explains its appeal.

We begin with some simple examples illustrating the supervenience of truth.

1. Illustrations of Supervenience

Consider our old favorite: the proposition that snow is white. As a matter of fact, snow is white, and because snow is white, <Snow is white> is true. Because <Snow is white> is true, <<Snow is white> is true> is also true, and so on. The explanatory chain begins with the fact that snow is white and proceeds through the hierarchy of truth-iterations, each link in the chain being secured by the combination of the link immediately preceding it and a truth-equivalence of the form <<p> is true iff p>, which serves to interlock them. Thus, we have:

---

[7] In this chapter, to keep things simple, I ignore truth-like properties other than truth and falsity *(e.g., being true of* and *being false of)*. The account of truth I present in this chapter may be expanded into an account of other truth-like properties.

[8] Here again, to be absolutely general, one would need to include other truth-like properties such as *being true of* and *being false of*.

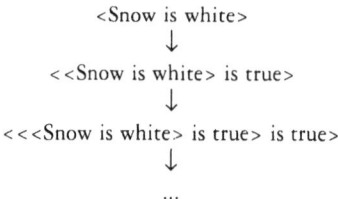

The determination in question is transitive. Since <Snow is white> determines its first truth-iteration, and the first iteration determines the second, *etc.,* <Snow is white> determines each of its truth-iterations.

In this example, then, there exists a chain of dependencies, extending from a truth-free proposition throughout the hierarchy of its truth-iterations. The iterations are true because they are determined by the true, truth-free proposition that snow is white. The same is true, of course, for <Foxes are furry> and its truth-iterations; each of its iterations is true because it is determined by the truth-free truth <Foxes are furry>. What these two sets of truth-iterations have in common, then, can be summarized like this: each of their members is true because it is determined by a true, truth-free ancestor (under the inverse of Tr (*i.e.*, Tr⁻¹).

Three distinct "because"-claims are in order for each truth-iteration of <Snow is white>. Thus, for the first iteration, we have

(i) <<Snow is white> is true> is true because it is determined by a true, truth-free ancestor under Tr⁻¹>.

(ii) <<Snow is white> is true> is true because it is determined by the truth-free truth <Snow is white>.

(iii) <<Snow is white> is true> is true because snow is white.

(i) - (iii) do not compete, nor do they jointly entail any "over-determination" of the fact that <<Snow is true> is true> . Compare an analogous trio of claims concerning a person whose bloodline traces to the Alamo (the battle of the Alamo, that is):

(2i) Smith's bloodline traces to the Alamo because he is a descendent of someone who was present at the Alamo.

(2ii) Smith's bloodline traces to the Alamo because he is a descendent of Davy Crockett.

(2iii) Smith's bloodline traces to the Alamo because Davy Crockett lived.

The combination of (2i) - (2iii) is clearly unproblematic, and so likewise is that of (i) - (iii). (i) and (2i) are (at least in part) analytic claims, respectively, about *what it is* for <<Snow is white> is true> to be true and *what it is* for Smith's bloodline to trace to the Alamo. Moreover, they cite determinable *analysantia*. It is natural then that we should cite explanations in terms of the determinates of these determinables. There may be problems of "explanatory exclusion" involving certain natural-seeming "because"-claims, but nothing of the kind is to be found in connection with the combination of (i) - (iii) or that of (2i) - (2iii).

So we have our first hints toward a treatment of the liar-like pathologies: truth-free propositions determine all their truth-iterations, and what it is for any such iteration to be true is for it to be determined by its truth-free ancestor under Tr^{-1}.

Now let us look beyond truth-iterations to other cases of supervenience or determination. Suppose I entertain at 1:00 exactly one proposition, the proposition <<Snow is white> is true>. And suppose this proposition is commonly entertained at that time. Then the fact that some proposition I entertain at 1:00 is true and the fact that some proposition commonly entertained at 1:00 is true are involved in determination chains that can be traced to the fact that snow is white. In the former case, we have

The chain of determination of the fact that some proposition I entertain at 1:00 is true

<Snow is white & at 1:00, I entertain <<Snow is white> is true>>
↓
<<Snow is white> is true & at 1:00, I entertain <<Snow is white> is true>>
↓
<SOME PROPOSITION I ENTERTAIN AT 1:00 IS TRUE>

↓
<<Some proposition I entertain at 1:00 is true> is true>
↓
<<<Some proposition I entertain at 1:00 is true> is true> is true>
↓
...

The entries which would replace the dots would denote truth-iterations on <Some proposition I entertain at 1:00 is true>.

In the case of <Some proposition commonly entertained at 1:00 is true>, there are no doubt many chains of determination. Here is one:

A chain of determination of the fact that some proposition commonly entertained at 1:00 is true

<Snow is white & at 1:00, <<Snow is white> is true> is commonly entertained>
↓
<<Snow is white> is true & at 1:00, <<Snow is white> is true> is commonly entertained>
↓
<SOME PROPOSITION COMMONLY ENTERTAINED AT 1:00 IS TRUE>

↓
<<Some proposition commonly entertained at 1:00 is true> is true>
↓
<<<Some proposition commonly entertained at 1:00 is true> is true> is true>
↓
...

So long as an F is determined, the existential <There is a true F> is guaranteed to be determined. The upshot of our considerations is therefore this: an existential truth-generalization is determined in the way required for truth iff at least one of its instances is so determined. Determination is transferred from instance to existential generalization.

The determination relations in the existential cases are importantly different from those we observed in the case of the simple truth-iterations on <Snow is white>. In the existential cases, the fact that snow is white does not *itself* determine the facts <Some proposition I entertain at 1:00 is true> and <Some proposition commonly entertained at 1:00 is true>, even if these meet the description in question. Rather, the determination is accomplished by instances of the generalizations, and the instances themselves are then determined in both cases by a conjunction one conjunct of which is the fact that snow is white, the other being a fact that identifies a truth-attributing proposition—*a truth-identificatory fact*, or for short, an *identificatory* fact. The relevant identificatory facts, respectively, are the fact that at 1:00 I entertain <<Snow is white> is true> and the fact that at 1:00 <<Snow is white> is true> is commonly entertained.

What is it in general for a proposition to be identificatory? Roughly, a proposition is identificatory iff it involves truth but does not *predicatively involve truth*.[9] For the time being, let us leave the notion of *predicatively involving truth* intuitive; suffice it to say that if a proposition involves truth *only* insofar as it *identifies or picks out* some other proposition involving truth—as in <The proposition I entertain at 1:00 = <Snow is white> is true>>—then it does not predicatively involve truth.

Now let us consider universal truth-generalizations. Given our previous definition of "attributing truth," propositions such as <Everything Bill Clinton says is true> do not count as truth-attributing. Nor (arguably) do they even broadly entail contingent propositions attributing truth. <Everything Bill Clinton said is true> would have been true if Bill Clinton had been mute. But whether or not such universal generalizations entail attributions of truth, their disjunctive cousins clearly do not; witness <Everything is such that either Bill Clinton did not say it or it is true>. In general, though, universal truth-generalizations seem to depend for their truth, no less than their existential cousins, on their standing in determination relations to (parts of) the totality of truth-free and identificatory fact.

Consider the schematic case of <Everything S said is true>, where S said only that snow is white and that foxes are furry.[10] We have the chain of determination:

Chain of determination for the fact that everything S said is true

<Snow is white & foxes are furry & for all P, S said P iff P = <Foxes are furry>
v P = <Snow is white>>
↓

---

[9] I use 'predicatively involving truth' as short for 'predicatively involving truth, falsity, being not true, being not false'.

[10] Schematic letters such as 'S' and 'F', let us say, may accept only names (predicates) of English that do not involve the predicates 'true' or 'false' (or 'is true of', *etc.*).

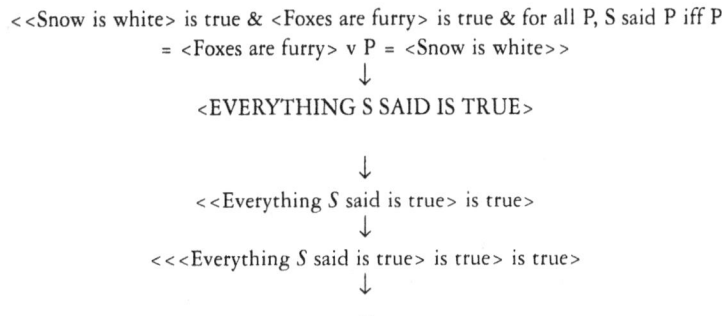

It is unclear whether *all* true universal truth-generalizations are determined in this way. Consider a generalization about *all* propositions, e.g., <For all x, if x is a proposition, then x is not both true and false>. It seems this generalization is determined in part (if not in whole) by each of its instances. But is there a conjunctive proposition, conjoining each such instance *and* an FIP ("full inventory proposition") which asserts in effect that "no entity other that...and...and...is a proposition"? If there is, the FIP in question would have to include itself in the list. But are there propositions that are about themselves directly?

This is an intriguing question, but one we need not answer here. We may affirm a weak claim concerning all universal truth-generalizations: a universal truth-generalization is determined iff each of its instances is determined. Here again, as in connection with existential truth-generalizations, we speak not of generalizations *being determined by* some one true proposition but as simply *being determined*. We swap the transitive verb for the intransitive.

The instances of some universal or existential truth-generalizations are themselves truth-generalizations. So it looks as if we need a recursive theory of determination. I will have more to say about this later. For now, though, I hope you see the emergence of a pattern. On the one hand, we have the totality of truth-free and identificatory propositions, whose truth or falsity is a deflationary matter, and on the other, we have propositions that require for their truth foundation in the totality of truth-free fact. A proposition is so founded iff it is determined. We may say, then, as a "second stab," that truth for the truth-free and the identificatory is deflationary, and that truth for other propositions consists in being determined.

This is progress. However, the categorization of propositions into *the truth-free*, *the identificatory*, and *the remainders* needs clarification and motivation if it is to serve as the basis for a perfectly general account of truth. We need to answer questions such as these: Are complex propositions whose components mix truth-free and identificatory propositions themselves identificatory? Are they remainders? Are some identificatory and others remainders? This focuses attention on the question, 'How are we to understand the notion of *predicatively involving truth*?' As for motivation, we must answer one question in particular, 'Why should truth for each and every remainder—given our identification of the remainders—be a dependent matter?' It is perhaps clear that truth for truth-attributing propositions is a dependent matter;

but what of truth for propositions such as <<Snow is white> is true iff snow is white>?

II. CATEGORIAL PRELIMINARIES

Let us begin by putting labels on our problems. Let us work with an exhaustive categorization of propositions into the *truth-independent* and the *truth-dependent*. To clarify these categories is to clarify what it is about a proposition that qualifies it as a candidate *either* for deflationary truth or falsity (in which case it is truth-independent) *or* for truth or falsity by virtue of determination (in which case it is truth-dependent). This section aims to provide the needed clarification.

I will proceed as follows: first, I will focus on the clearest cases of truth-independent propositions, the truth-free and the identificatory, explaining as best I can what precisely I mean when I say that a proposition is identificatory, and specifying the truth-independent propositions by reference to these clearest cases; second, I will justify counting as truth-dependent all other propositions, all the remainders.

Truth- and falsity-free propositions—propositions that involve neither of these, either predicatively or otherwise—are obviously truth-independent. So, also, are identificatory propositions. For <At 1:00, I entertain <<Snow is white> is true> to be true is just for me to be such that at 1:00 I entertain <<Snow is white> is true>. Earlier, I said that identificatory propositions involve truth but do not *predicatively involve truth*, suggesting that mere reference to proposition involving truth was insufficient for predicatively involving truth. I now elaborate. Intuitively, we might say this: a proposition predicatively involves truth in the first instance iff to believe it is to attribute a truth-like property to something. Less intuitively, we might then go on to assert that a proposition derivatively predicatively involves truth iff its truth or falsity would need to be determined by the truth of some proposition predicatively involving truth in the first instance, that is, iff the proposition can be gotten from a proposition non-derivatively predicatively involving truth by the application of logical operation. The basic idea would then be that to predicatively involve truth is *either* to attribute or deny truth or falsity *or* to bear narrow logical relations to some proposition that does.

These thoughts can be made more precise by the following recursive characterization of *predicatively involving truth*.

A proposition P predicatively involves truth iff *either*

    (i)   P is itself a value of Tr, Neg-Tr, Fls, or Neg-Fls for some argument
           (*e.g.*, <<Snow is white> is true>)

or

    (ii)   P is the value of one of the logical forms for an argument that predicatively involves truth
           (*e.g.*, <If <Snow is white> is true, then snow is white>, <For all P, P is true>, <Possibly, <Snow is blue> is true>)

or

(iii)   P is a proposition that *trivially* or *analytically* entails or is trivially or analytically entailed by a proposition predicatively involving truth
(*e.g.*, <Tr(<Snow is white>) entails <Snow is white>>, which trivially entails <If <Snow is white> is true, then snow is white>; <Oscar knows that snow is white>, which analytically entails <<Snow is white> is true>; <Jones's desire that the Jets win the Superbowl is unfulfilled>, which analytically entails <<The Jets win the Superbowl> is not true>)

or

(iv)   P is the value of one of the logical forms of generality (*i.e.*, UG, EG) applied to a propositional function, which in turn, is applied to a proposition predicatively involving truth for some argument
(*e.g.*, <Everything Oscar said is true>, <Everything Oscar said is true iff <<Snow is white> is true>)

This gives us plausible results. Among propositions counted as predicatively involving truth are these:

<Snow is white & (If grass is green, then something is true)>
<Every proposition expressed in the *U.S. Constitution* is true>
<<Snow is white> is true iff snow is white>
<Every proposition Oscar said is necessarily equivalent to <<Snow is white> is true>>

The last entry on the list is counted as predicatively involving truth because propositions of the form <<*p*> is necessarily equivalent to Tr(<*q*>)> trivially entail their cousins of the form <*p* iff <*q*> is true>.

With the notion of *predicatively involving truth* intact, let us resolve to count propositions as identificatory iff they involve truth but do not predicatively involve truth. This seems give us just what we want: identificatory propositions involve truth only because they make *reference* to truth, whether directly, as in <Truth is a property>, or indirectly by making reference to propositions involving truth., as in <Fred said <<Snow is white> is true>>.

We are now ready to give our account of *the truth-independent* and *the truth-dependent*:

For all propositions P, P is *truth-independent* iff P is either truth-free or identificatory

For all propositions P, P is *truth-dependent* iff P is not truth-independent

Finally, the metacategorial concern: why should all propositions that predicatively involve truth, including the remainders (which neither attribute nor deny truth or falsity) be counted truth-dependent? Propositions that attribute truth (or deny truth, *etc.*) are rightly counted truth-dependent, as is plain from the illustrations of determination in the last section, but what of the rest?

Molecular combinations and generalizations from propositions attributing truth depend for their truth-status (*i.e.*, their status as true, false, not true, not false)

on that of their components, and so are rightly counted truth-dependent. That, I think, is clear. But what of molecular combinations drawing from the truth-free and the truth-attributing? These should be counted among the truth-dependent because they are at least *formally dependent* for some aspect of their truth-status on the truth-status of their truth-attributing components. Take, for example, the disjunction <Snow is white v <Grass is red> is true>. This proposition is true in fact owing to the truth of its disjunct <Snow is white>. It might have been true owing to the truth of <<Grass is red> is true>, *e.g.*, in a world in which snow is not white but grass is red. But even in the actual world we can say that the disjunction is of such a form that it *would* depend for its status as false on the statuses of its disjuncts. *Mutatis mutandis* for conjunctions whose conjuncts mix the truth-free and the truth-attributing, and for truth-generalizations whose instances mix these sources. (Recall that <Everything S said is true> is patently truth-dependent and that its instances are trivially equivalent to disjunctions mixing the truth-free and the truth-attributing, *e.g.*, <S did not say that snow is white & <Snow is white> is true>.)

By a further step, closure conditions seem justifiable: a disjunction is truth-dependent if one of its disjuncts is, a conjunction truth-dependent if one of its conjuncts is, a negation truth-dependent if its contradictory is, an existential or universal generalization truth-dependent if its instances are. A disjunction *would* depend for its falsity on the falsity of both of its disjuncts; a conjunction *would* depend for its truth on the truth of both of its conjuncts, and so on. Finally, any proposition that analytically or trivially entails a truth-dependent proposition *would* depend for its falsity on that of the truth-dependent propositions it entails.

If the totality of truth-dependent propositions fulfills these conditions, it is identical to the totality of propositions that predicatively involve truth.

III. An (Almost) General Account of Truth

We now turn to the task of providing a general account of truth. Our guiding idea is that truth for some propositions—the truth-independent propositions—is deflationary whereas truth for the remainders—the truth-dependent propositions—consists in being determined. But how should we think of determination?

An initially attractive thought is that determination consists in broad entailment by the totality of truth-independent facts. Perhaps there is no *set* of all truth-independent facts, but there might still be an entity worth calling "the totality of truth-independent fact". Our analyses of truth and falsity for truth-dependent propositions would then take the form of a supervenience principle:

> Necessarily, for all truth-dependent propositions P, P is true iff P is broadly entailed by some part of the totality of truth-independent fact, and P is false iff Neg(P) is broadly entailed by some part of that same totality.

This would then be supplemented with a deflationary account of truth and falsity for truth-independent propositions and principles concerning the transference of truth under truth-iteration and the incompatibility of truth and falsity:

For all truth-independent *P*, *P* is broadly equivalent to Tr(*P*), and Neg(*P*) is broadly equivalent to Fls(*P*).

For all propositions *P*, Tr(*P*) is broadly equivalent to Tr(Tr(*P*)).

For all propositions *P*, Tr(*P*) broadly entails Neg(Fls(*P*)), and Fls(*P*) broadly entails Neg(Tr(*P*)).

Unfortunately, the simple account is unacceptable. Even if the needed notion of a *totality* could be satisfactorily explained, there is a deeper problem. In addressing the liar-like pathologies, we must be prepared to part with principles about truth that we find pretheoretically plausible. Some principles, however, are dearer to us than others. One that is very dear is the principle of *the transference of truth under analytic entailment*, viz. that where *P* analytically entails *Q*, if *P* is true, then *Q* is true as well. The simple account does not sustain this principle. For suppose <The *F* is not true> is pathological (with the *F* = <The *F* is not true>) and so counted neither true nor false insofar as the totality of truth-independent fact, TIF, fails to broadly entail either it or its negation. If this is so, it is *necessarily* so. So *every* proposition broadly entails

(4)   <Not-(TIF broadly entails <The *F* is not true>)>

Thus, TIF itself broadly entails (4). But TIF presumably also broadly entails with respect to itself that it is the totality of truth-independent fact. (TIF, after all, is maximal in the sense that for every truth-independent proposition, either that proposition itself or its negation is part of TIF. TIF will therefore include in its ranks the proposition that TIF is maximal in this sense. Given, then, that TIF broadly entails both its own truth and its own maximality, it broadly entails that it is a maximal totality of truth-independent fact. Necessarily, there can be only one such totality.[11] Consequently, TIF broadly entails (5):

(5)   <TIF is the totality of truth-independent fact & Not-(TIF broadly entails <The F is not true>)>

If the account of truth based on the simple theory of determination is correct, then, (5) is true. But (5) analytically entails <<The *F* is not true> is not true>. So by the principle about analytic entailment, <<The *F* is not true> is not true> is true. But the latter is not true. If it were, then since the *F* = <The *F* is not true>, the *F* itself would turn out true. This would give us the contradictory conclusion: the *F* is true (since <the *F* is not true> is determined by TIF), and the *F* is not true (since it is undetermined by TIF).

The problem stems from the promiscuity of broad entailment. Insofar as there is or is not a relation of broad entailment between a pair of propositions, this is a

---

[11] Suppose that in addition to TIF, TIF* is such a totality. Both TIF and TIF* are true. Given the simple account, all the parts of TIF and TIF* are true. But TIF has a part Q that is incompatible with some part R of TIF*. So the negation of the conjunction of Q and R is necessary. But since that conjunction is necessarily equivalent to the proposition with respect to it that it is true, the negation of the latter proposition is also necessary.

broadly necessary fact, and so every proposition will broadly entail it. In other words, by making broad entailment the measure of determination, one commits oneself to the existence of truths about determination or the lack of determination *for every proposition*, including pathological propositions. If the principle about analytic entailment is then retained, contradiction arises in the case of the <The F is not true> where this *is* the F.

We do better to explain determination in terms of a more restrictive relation to the realm of truth-independent fact. One might try to explain it in terms of narrow entailment in conjunction with select truth-equivalences and falsity-equivalences, but I shall try a different tack. In our discussion of the determination of the truth-iterations of <Snow is white> and of truth-generalizations, we hinted at a recursive treatment of determination. An existential truth-generalization, we said, is determined iff at least one of its instances is, a universal truth-generalization iff each of its instances is.

Following this lead, I propose the following general account of truth:

General account of truth: (FMT-G)

Part I: Propositional truth for truth-independent propositions:
For all propositions P, if P is truth-independent, then P is broadly equivalent to Tr(P) and Neg(P) is broadly equivalent to Fls(P)

Part II: Propositional truth for truth-dependent propositions:
For all truth-dependent propositions P, necessarily, P is true iff P is determined, and P is false iff Neg(P) is determined

Part III: Truth for non-propositional entities:
For all non-propositional objects o, o is true iff x expresses a true proposition, and o is false iff o expresses a false proposition

Part IV: The mutual exclusivity of propositional truth and truth for non-propositional entities:
Only propositions can have propositional truth or falsity. No proposition can have truth for non-propositional entities

(FMT-G) can be briefly summarized:

Part I: Truth (falsity) for truth-independent propositions is deflationary

Part II: Truth (falsity) for truth-dependent propositions consists in determination (determination of the negation)

Part III: Truth (falsity) for non-propositional truth-bearers consists in the expression of true (false) propositions

Part IV: Only propositions can have propositional truth or falsity; propositions cannot have truth for non-propositional entities

The Liar Paradox

Necessary and sufficient conditions for truth-independence and truth-dependence of propositions have already been given. We now want to give a recursive account of determination. Moreover, we want the account to conform to certain "truth-rules", rules which allow us to move stepwise from the realm of truth-independent fact through the realm of truth-dependent fact, rules which allow us to trace the chains of determination of truth-dependent propositions. The following, albeit partial, is a working list:

Schematic rule for truth-independent propositions:
Where <p> is truth-independent, count true <p> just in case p

Rule for non-propositional entities that do not express propositions:
Where o neither is nor expresses a proposition, count true <o is not true> and <o is not false>.

Rules for propositions attributing or denying truth or falsity:
Where P is true, count true Tr(P), Neg-Fls(P)
Where Neg(P) is true, count true Fls(P) and Neg-Tr(P)
Where o expresses a truth, count true Tr(o), Neg-Fls(o)
Where o expresses the negation of a truth, count true Fls(o), and Neg-Tr(o)

Rule for disjunctions:
Where P is true, count true any disjunction containing P as a disjunct

Rule for conjunctions:
Where P and Q are true, count true their conjunction

Rule for existential generalizations:
Where an instance of an existential generalization is true, count true the generalization

Rule for universal generalizations:
Where every instance of a universal generalization is true, count true the generalization

Taken together with (FMT-G), the rules above concerning molecular propositions and generalizations have the defect that they are redundant in their application to truth-independent truths. Furthermore, we want our account to apply to propositions trivially or analytically equivalent to the various sorts of proposition mentioned in our truth-rules. For example, we want to count true <Not-(not-p & not-q)> just in case we count true <p v q>. Finally, we want to insure that nothing is counted true other than those propositions the truth-rules (suitably modified) instruct us to count true.[12] To these ends, I propose the following recursive account of determination:

---

[12] To accommodate propositions attributing necessity and possibility, we may treat <<p> is necessary> as equivalent to <For every world w, in w, p> and <<p> is possible> as equivalent to <For some world w, in w, p>. We may then provide rules parallel to the above:

(Determination)

Necessarily, for all propositions P, P is determined iff P is a truth-dependent proposition and either:

 (i) P is the value of Neg-Tr (or Neg-Fls) for a non-propositional object *o* that does not express a proposition

or

 (ii) P is the value of Tr (or Neg-Fls) for a proposition Q that is either a truth-independent truth or determined

or

 (iii) P is the value of Fls (or Neg-Tr) for a proposition Q whose negation is either a truth-independent truth or determined

or

 (iv) P is the value of Tr (or Neg-Fls) for a non-propositional entity x

---

Rule for non-propositional entities:
 Where x is not a proposition and W is any world, count true <In W, x is not true> and <In W, x is not false>.

Rules for propositions attributing or denying truth or falsity:
 Where P is true in world W, count true <In W, P is true> and <In W, P is not false>
 Where Neg(P) is true in a world W, count true <In W, P is false>, and <In W, P is not true>.
 Where x expresses a truth in world W, count true both <In W, x is true> and <In W, x is not false>.
 Where x expresses the negation of a truth in world W, count true both <In W, x is false> and <In W, x is not true>.

Rule for disjunctions:
 Where P is true in a world W, count true any disjunction containing as a disjunct the value of the function <In w, p> for the argument pair (W, P).
 Example: where <Snow is white> is true in W, count true <In W, snow is white v the Jets won the Superbowl in 1995>

Rule for conjunctions:
 Where P and Q are true in a world W, count true the conjunction whose conjuncts are the values of <In w, p> for the pairs (W, P) and (W, Q).
 Example: where <Snow is white> and <Rain is wet> are true in W, count true <In W, snow is white & rain is wet>

Rule for existential generalizations:
 Where an instance P of an existential generalization is true in a world W, count true the existential generalization of the value of <In w, p> for the pair (W, P).
 Example: where <Snow is white> is true in W, count true <In W, there is something that is white>

Rule for universal generalizations:
 Where every instance P of a universal generalization is true, count true the universal generalization of the value of <In w, p> for the pair (W, P) the generalization.
 Example: where every value of <If x is a human being, then x is mortal> is true in W, count true <In W, every human being is mortal>.

Finally, rules for necessity and possibility:

Rules for attributions of necessity and possibility:
 Where for every world W, the value of <In w, p> for pair (W, P) is true, count true <P is necessary>
 Where for at least one world W, the value of <In w, p> for pair (W, P) is true, count true <P is possible>

The Liar Paradox

> that expresses a proposition that is either a truth-independent
> truth or determined
>
> *or*
> (v)   *P* is the value of either Fls (or Neg-Tr) for a non-propositional
>   entity *x* that expresses a proposition whose negation is either a
>   truth-independent truth or determined
>
> *or*
> (vi)   *P* is a disjunction at least one of whose disjuncts is either a
>   truth-independent truth or determined
>
> *or*
> (vii) *P* is a conjunction both of whose conjuncts is either a truth-
>   independent truth or determined
>
> *or*
> (viii) *P* is an existential generalization at least one of whose instances
>   is determined
>
> *or*
> (ix)   *P* is a universal generalization each of whose instances is deter-
>   mined
>
> *or*
> (x)   *P* is trivially or analytically entailed by a proposition that is
>   determined.

Redundancy is eliminated, since we require that a proposition be truth-dependent to be determined. Clause (x) comprehends trivial and analytic consequences of true propositions. And our account—if suitably enriched to take account of other kinds of propositions—states necessary and sufficient conditions for determination, thus fulfilling the requirement that only those propositions which our truth-rules instructs us to declare true are declared true.[13] [14] Given that (Determination) itself

---

[13] Two qualifying comments regarding (Determination). (1) (Determination) may only approximate the truth about determination; further clauses perhaps need to be added in (Determination); (2) I assume, for simplicity's sake, that a conditional IF(*P, Q*) is trivially equivalent to DISJ(Neg(*P*), *Q*), that a biconditional IFF(*P, Q*) is trivially equivalent to the conjunction of the relevant disjunctions, and that De Morgan equivalents are trivially equivalent.

[14] We might try to bring propositions involving necessity and possibility into the fold as follows. We begin by adding the counterparts of clauses (i), (ii), and (iii) for propositions about worlds:

> *P* is the value of the function <In world *w*, *x* is not true> for a pair (*W, o*),
> where *o* is not a proposition.
>
> *P* is the value of <In world *w*, <*p*> is true>, for a pair (*W, Q*), where *W*
> is a world and *Q* is a proposition, and the value of <In world *w, p*> for this
> pair is either a truth-independent truth or determined.
>
> *P* is the value of <In world *w*, <*p*> is false>, for a pair (*W, Q*), where *W*
> is a world and *Q* is a proposition, and the negation of the value of <In
> world *w, p*> for this pair is either a truth-independent truth or determined.

Corresponding to clauses (iv) - (ix)), we would have clauses about truth in worlds for non-propositional entities, for disjunctions, conjunctions, and generalizations. Finally, for attributions of necessity and possibility, we would have:

lacks the richness we must have, it will not supply the basis for a completely general account of truth. Strictly speaking, therefore, (FMT-G) can only be called "almost general."

(Determination) is admittedly not as simple as the simple account in terms of broad entailment. Nonetheless, it too sustains an intuitive supervenience principle for truth and falsity:

(Supervenience)

Intuitively: There can be no difference in truth-value of truth-dependent propositions without a difference in truth-value of truth-independent propositions

More precisely: There are no distinct broadly possible worlds W and W' such that W and W' agree on truth-value of all truth-independent propositions but disagree on truth-value of a truth-dependent proposition

According to (FMT-G) (supplemented with (Determination)[15]) the truth-values of truth-dependent propositions are fixed by the truth-values of truth-independent propositions. This fits well with our invocation of the truth-rules: the truth-rules, supplemented with the meta-rule that "nothing else is to be counted true (false)" collectively require on our part sameness of truth-value assignments for the truth-dependent given sameness of truth-value assignments for the truth-independent.

Let us put (FMT-G) to the test by considering the paradigm pathological cases: the strengthened liar, the original liar, the truth-teller, and the sentential versions of these.

The strengthened liar: Suppose the F = <The F is not true>. What is the truth-status of <The F is not true>?

This proposition is truth-dependent, but neither it nor its negation is determined. The determination-status (*i.e.*, the status of being determined or being undetermined) of a proposition of the form <The F is not true>, whether a liar or not, depends on that of the F. If the F is undetermined, <The F is not true> is undetermined. If the negation of the F is undetermined, the negation of <The F is not true> is undetermined. So in the present case, where the F = <The F is not true>, we are left with a circle: <The F is not true> is determined iff the F is determined iff <The F is not true> is determined. No contact is made between the circle and the realm of truth-independent fact. Thus, given (FMT-G), <The F is not true> is counted untrue. So, too, is its negation, <Not-(the F is not true)>. Since there is just one F,

---

P is the value of the propositional function <x is necessary> for some proposition Q as argument, and for every world W, the value of the function <In w, p> for the pair (W, Q) is determined.

P is the value of the propositional function <x is possible> for some proposition Q as argument, and for some world W, the value of the function <In w, p> for the pair (W, Q) is determined.

[15] For simplicity, let us use '(FMT-G)' to denote the combination of (FMT-G), (Determination), the account of truth-dependence and truth-independence.

The Liar Paradox 117

<Not-(the *F* is not true> is determined iff <The *F* is true>—the truth-teller—is determined. But, under (FMT-G), propositions of the form <The *F* is true> depend for their determination-status on that of the *F*. So, again, we have a circle of potential determination unconnected to the realm of truth-independent fact. Both <The *F* is true> and <Not-(the *F* is not true)> are undetermined. Consequently, under (FMT-G), the strengthened liar is neither true nor false.[16]

The circular element in this case can perhaps be most easily appreciated if we think of the principles of determination specified in (Determination) as *rules*. In the case of the strengthened liar, SL, the rules tell us only that SL is determined iff SL is determined. We are forbidden from judging SL determined on the basis of our judgments concerning the truth-independent facts. When we turn to the negation of the strengthened liar, our rules tell us that -SL is determined iff SL is determined. Thus, (FMT-G) demands we conclude that SL is neither true nor false.

Note, finally, that where <The *F* is not true> is a strengthened liar, it is not the case that <The *F* is not true> is true iff the *F* is not true. For <The *F* is not true> is not true even while the *F* is not true. (After all, the *F* = <The *F* is not true>). Thus, (FMT-G) enables us to block the paradoxical conclusion that troubled us at the start of this chapter. Where the proposition I entertain at 1:00 = <The proposition I entertain at 1:00 is not true>, we cannot use <<The proposition I entertain at 1:00 is not true> is true iff the proposition I entertain at 1:00 is not true> to derive a paradox.

---

[16] My treatment might seem too swift. Let us, then, consider the matter in more detail. Suppose we give <The *F* is not true> a Russellian interpretation. So we count this proposition as being identical with the proposition <There is a *y* such that for all *x*, *x* is *F* iff *x*=*y* & *y* is not true>. What is the truth-status of our proposition, then? Since we are dealing with an existential generalization, we must ask whether it has an instance that is determined. Each of its instances is a universal truth-generalization. So we must ultimately look to see whether each of its instances is determined. The problematic instance is this:

(1)   <<The *F* is not true> is *F* iff (<The *F* is not true> = <The *F* is not true> & <The *F* is not true> is not true)>

Since (1) is a biconditional, we must ask whether its "left-hand" and "right-hand" propositions are determined (or truth-independent truths). The "left-hand" proposition of (1) is obviously true: <The *F* is not true> = the *F*. The "right-hand" proposition is determined only if its conjunct <<The *F* is not true> is not true> is determined. But, given the identity of the *F*, we know that the latter is determined only if <The *F* is not true> is determined. But now we're back to where we started! There is a *circle* of potential determination, but the circle does not connect to the realm of the truth-independent fact.

What of the negation of <The *F* is not true>, *i.e.*, <Not-(the *F* is not true)>? This is analytically equivalent to a universal truth-generalization. Following the guidelines specified in (Determination), we see that <Not-(the *F* is not true)> is determined only if <<The *F* is not true> is true> is determined. But the latter is determined only if the strengthened liar itself —<The *F* is not true>—is determined. The truth-status of the negation of the strengthened liar depends on that of the strengthened liar. Since the strengthened liar is undetermined, so too is its negation.

We may conclude that, given (FMT-G), <The *F* is not true> is neither true nor false.

The liar. Suppose the F = <The F is false>. What is the status of <The F is false>?

Here, too, the proposition in question is truth-dependent, but there is no truth-independent truth that determines it or its negation.[17] In general, propositions of the form <The F is false> depend for their determination-status on that of the negation of the F. In the present case, then, <The F is false> depends for its determination-status on that of <Not-(the F is false)>. Given that there is exactly one F, we arrive at the conclusion that <The F is false> is determined iff <The F is not false> is determined. By the same sort of reasoning as we used in the case of the strengthened liar, we can see that <The F is not false> can admit of only circular determination, and so is undetermined. Thus, following (FMT-G), we conclude that the liar is neither true nor false.

Interestingly, where <The F is false> is a liar, we do reach the result that <The F is false> is true iff the F is false. For <The F is false> is not true, and the F (*viz.* <The F is false>) is not false. How, then, is paradox blocked? The reasoning we must block is this:

(6) <The F is false> is true iff the F is false
∴ (7) The F is true iff the F is false
∴ (8) The F is true iff the F is not true

Since we allow (6), we must question either the step to (7) or the step to (8). The step to (7) is justified by the identity of the F and <The F is false>. The step to (8), however, relies on an unrestricted principle of bivalence, which is plainly inconsistent with the existence of liars, given (FMT-G). ((7) might seem troubling. But it turns out to be quite innocent. The F is true iff the F is false just insofar as the F is neither true nor false.)

The truth-teller. Suppose the F = <The F is true>. What is the truth-status of <The F is true>?

Our diagnosis here follows our diagnoses in the previous cases. Where <The F is true> = the F, <The F is true> depends for its determination-status on the F, and so is undetermined. Its negation, <Not-(the F is true)>, depends for its determination-status on that of <The F is not true>, which in turn depends for its determination-status on that of the F. The truth-teller is therefore neither true nor false, given (FMT-G).

The Sentential Strengthened Liar, Truth-Teller, and Liar. Each of the sentential paradigm cases has a parallel in the paradigm propositional cases. So I will consider only the

---

[17] A variant of a case described by Kripke (1975) can be treated similarly. Suppose Jones says <Everything Nixon said about Watergate is false>, but that Nixon said <Everything Jones says about me (Nixon) is false>. We focus on both these propositions. Our desired result is that they both come out neither true nor false.

Regardless of what else Nixon and Jones say, the propositions <Everything Nixon said about Watergate is false> and <Everything Jones says about Nixon is false>, are undetermined; and the same goes for their negations. So, these come out as neither true nor false.

case of the sentential strengthened liar. Extrapolations to the other cases are easily made.

Suppose A names 'A is not true'. What is the truth-status of A under (FMT-G)? By Part II of (FMT-G), A is true iff A expresses a true proposition. What A expresses is the truth-independent proposition <A is not true>. Again we find a circle of potential determination: <A is not true> is determined iff what A expresses (*i.e.*, <A is not true>) is determined. So <A is not true> is undetermined, and A is not true. (Compare the case in which A names "'Snow is white' is true." Then A comes out true because what A expresses, <'Snow is white' is true> is determined. The latter is determined because 'Snow is white' expresses the truth-independent truth that snow is white.) The negation of <A is not true>, *i.e.*, <A is true>, too, is unable to receive determination, since it depends for its determination-status on that of <A is not true>, which is undetermined. As a result, A is counted neither true nor false under (FMT-G).

I submit that these are desirable results. In defense of the truth-teller results, which perhaps are the least obvious of the group, we can say this: we cannot understand how <The F is true> could be true or false when it is a truth-teller; if the truth-teller had a truth-value, it would have do so in the absence of foundation in the truth-independent facts. No chain of determination would link the totality of truth-independent fact to the truth-teller or to its negation.

I propose that *pathology* for propositions consists in being an truth-dependent proposition that itself is undetermined and whose negation is also undetermined. This claim comports well with the paradigm cases of pathology. It will be assumed throughout that the pathological propositions are the truth-dependent propositions that meet the conditions just given. I leave it to the reader to judge the adequacy of this identification, but I ask that she judge only after observing its fruits.

(FMT-G) has some attractive *general* features, for example:

(A) (FMT-G) sustains bivalence for non-pathological propositions.
(B) (FMT-G) sustains the principle that nothing true is false.
(C) The standard three-valued truth-tables are sustained:

P	Neg(P)	P	Q	CONJ(P, Q)	P	Q	DISJ(P, Q)
T	F	T	T	T	T	T	T
N	N	T	N	N	T	N	T
F	T	T	F	F	T	F	T
		N	T	N	N	T	T
		N	N	N	N	N	N
		N	F	F	N	F	N
		F	T	F	F	T	T
		F	N	F	F	N	N
		F	F	F	F	F	F

(D) (FMT-G) entails that every instance of Excluded Middle for a non-pathological proposition as argument is true.
(E) (FMT-G) entails principles of attachment for truth and falsity for non-pathological propositions. (That is, it entails:

(Attachment of truth)   For all non-pathological propositions P, if P is true, then $Tr(P)$ is true.
(Attachment of falsity)   For all non-pathological propositions P, if $Neg(P)$ is true, then $Fls(P))$ is true

(F) (FMT-G) entails principles of detachment for truth and falsity. (That is: It entails:

(Detachment of truth)   For all propositions P, if $Tr(P)$ is true, then P is true.
(Detachment of falsity)   For all propositions P, if $Fls(P)$ is true, then $Neg(P))$ is true.

(G) (FMT-G) entails that every value of the forms $<<p>$ is true iff $p>$ and $<<p>$ is false iff not-$p>$ for a non-pathological argument is true.
(H) (FMT-G) entails that for all P, $Tr(P)$ broadly entails P, and that for all P, $Fls(P)$ broadly entails $Neg(P)$.

For the less obvious claims among (A) - (H), I will offer demonstrations.

(A) is the claim that (FMT-G) sustains bivalence for non-pathological propositions. Given the identification of the pathological propositions with those undetermined truth-dependent propositions whose negations are undetermined, (A) trivially follows. However, behind the triviality, there lie important substantive truths: the pathology of *paradigm* pathological propositions consists in their being at once truth-dependent but such that neither they nor their negations are determined in the way required for truth or falsity; and the reason the paradigms fail in this regard is to be found not merely in their self-reference, but in their *indirect self-attribution or self-denial of truth or falsity*. These substantive truths about the nature of pathology, which explain and found our intuitions about the paradigm cases, justify further claims about pathology concerning non-paradigm cases. Pre-theoretic intuition is perhaps silent on whether the instances of Excluded Middle corresponding to pathological propositions are true. Our account of pathology bids us count them pathological as well. There is some intuitive justification for this extension: propositions that are not themselves paradigm cases of pathology but which depend on the paradigm cases for their status as true, false, or neither,—*e.g.*, propositions such as disjunctions of paradigm pathological propositions—would seem rightly counted as pathological by virtue of this dependence. But it is the plausibility of our account's treatment of the paradigm pathological cases that provides the strongest justification for its attributions of pathology to other propositions.

(B) is the claim that (FMT-G) yields the principle that nothing true is false. This principle is clearly sustained in the case of truth-independent propositions. The test case is that of truth-dependent propositions. We will have our proof if we can show that for any truth-dependent proposition P, if P is true, then $Neg(P)$ is not

The Liar Paradox

true. For, given the definition of falsity for truth-dependent propositions in terms of the determination of the negation, the latter would insure that if a truth-dependent proposition is true, it is not false. Our proof is an induction on the number of steps in a determination tree of a proposition. If a proposition is determined, there is at least one such tree. The first step in a determination tree is from the tips of the outer branches to their bases. The last step is to the target proposition.[18]

---

[18] Determination is step-wise, proceeding from proposition(s) to proposition by virtue of the application of clauses of (Determination), so we can number the steps, beginning with the tip, step 0, which consists entirely of truth-independent truths, non-propositional entities (such as sentences, utterances, as well as tables and chairs), and proceeding upwards. (This scheme presupposes that there is at most a countable number of steps in a determination tree. This is inessential. Transfinite induction could be used to secure more general results.)

For some propositions, there is more than one determination tree. Thus, in the case of <Everything S said is true>, where S said only
        <Snow is white>
        <<Grass is green> is true or rubies are red>
there are two trees:

```
                              TREE 1
Step 4                <Everything S said is true>
                       /                        \
Step 3   <S said <Snow is white> and <Snow is white> is true>    <S said <<Grass is green> is true
                                                                  or rubies are red> and <<Grass is
                                                                  green> is true or rubies are red> is
              /                \                                  true>
Step 2   <S said <Snow is white>     <Snow is white>       /                \
         <S said <<Grass is green> is true or rubies are red>   <<Grass is green> is true or rubies
                                                                 are red>
                                                                        \
Step 1                                                          <<Grass is green> is true>
                                                                        \
Step 0                                                          <Grass is green>

                              TREE 2
Step 3                <Everything S said is true>
                       /                        \
Step 2   <S said <Snow is white> and <Snow is white> is true>    <S said <<Grass is green> is true
                                                                  or rubies are red> and <<Grass is
                                                                  green> is true or rubies are red> is
              /                \                                  true>
Step 1   <S said <Snow is white>     <Snow is white>       /                \
         <S said <<Grass is green> is true or rubies are red>   <<Grass is green> is
                                                                 true or rubies are red>
                                                                        \
Step 0                                                          <Rubies are red>
```

Here is an example of a determination tree involving non-propositional entities. The tree, one would hope, is one of the many determination trees for the truth <A sentence of *Word and Object* is true>:

```
Step 3                    <A sentence of Word and Object is true>
                                         /
Step 2        <'Language is a social art' is a sentence of Word and Object and is true>
                       /                                    \
Step 1   <'Language is a social art' is            <'Language is a social art' is true>
         a sentence of Word and Object>
                                                      /                \
Step 0                                       'Language is a social art'   <Language is a social art>
```

The Base Case: Consider any proposition R, occurring at the first step in the determination tree of P. We must consider several possibilities. Possibility 1: R = Neg-Tr(o) or Neg-Fls(o) for an object o that neither is nor expresses a proposition. In this case Neg(R) is not determined, for no clause allows its determination and so it is not true. Possibility 2: R = Tr(Q_i) or Neg-Fls(Q_i) for some Q_i that is a truth-independent truth. In this case as well, Neg(R) is not true, since no clause allows its determination. Possibility 3: R = Fls(Q_i) or Neg-Tr(Q_i) for some Q_i the negation of which is a truth-independent truth. Here again, no clause allows the determination of Neg(R), and so it is not true. Possibility 4: R = Tr(x) or Neg-Fls(x) for some x that expresses a truth-independent truth. As before, we cannot reach the conclusion that Neg(R) is determined, and so it is not true. Possibility 5: R = Fls(x) or Neg-Fls(x) for some x that expresses a proposition the negation of which is a truth-independent truth. Again, Neg(R) is not determined, and so not true. Possibility 6: R = DISJ(Q_i,Q_j), where Q_i is a truth-independent truth. Neg(R) here trivially equivalent to CONJ(Neg(Q_i), Neg(Q_j)). But the clause for conjunction does not allow the determination of the latter. For since Neg(Q_i) is not true, CONJ(Neg(Q_i), Neg(Q_j)) is not determined, and so Neg(R) is not determined, and so not true. Possibility 7: R = CONJ(Q_i,Q_j), where both Q_i and Q_j are truth-independent truths. Neg(R) is trivially equivalent to DISJ(Neg(Q_i), Neg(Q_j)), but since neither Neg(Q_i) nor Neg(Q_j) is true, DISJ(Neg(Q_i), Neg(Q_j)) and Neg(R) are not determined, and the latter is not true.

The Base Case assures us that, where P is a truth-dependent truth, if P is determined in one step in some determination tree, then Neg(P) is not true.

The Inductive Step: We suppose that for any Q_i occurring at the nth step of a determination tree of P is such that Neg(Q_i) is not true. We show that the same holds for any proposition R, occurring at the $n+1$-th step of the same tree. Here there are nine possibilities to consider. Possibility 1: R = Tr(Q_i) or Neg-Fls(Q_i) for some truth-dependent truth Q_i occurring at the nth step. By hypothesis, Neg(Q_i) is not true. Now, Neg(R) is trivially equivalent to either Neg-Tr(Q_i) or Fls(Q_i). So, Neg(R) is not true, since the determination of the latter require that Neg(Q_i) be either determined or a truth-independent truth, which it is not. Possibility 2: R = Fls(Q_i) or Neg-Tr(Q_i) where Q_i occurs at the nth step. The case is the same, mutatis mutandis, as in Possibility 1. Possibility 3: R = Tr(x) or Neg-Fls(x) for some x that expresses a determined proposition Q_i, occurring at the nth step. By hypothesis, Q_i is true but Neg(Q_i) is not. But then Neg-Tr(Q_i) and Fls(Q_i) are not determined, and so their analytic equivalent Neg(R) is not determined, and so not true. Possibility 4: R = Fls(x) or Neg-Tr(x) for some x that expresses a proposition the negation of which, Q_i, is determined and occurs at the nth step. The case is the same, *mutatis mutandis*, as in Possibility 3. Possibility 5: R = DISJ(Q_i,Z) for some pair (Q_i,Z), where Q_i is determined and occurs at the nth step and Z is either truth-dependent or a truth-independent falsehood. By hypothesis, Neg(Q_i) is not determined. Now, Neg(R) is trivially equivalent to CONJ(Neg(Q_i), Neg(Z)), and the latter is determined iff both its conjuncts are determined, which they are not. So Neg(R) is not determined. Possibility 6: R = CONJ(Q_i,Q_j) for some pair (Q_i,Q_j), where Q_i and Q_j occur at the nth

The Liar Paradox

step. By hypothesis, Neg(Q_i) and Neg(Q_j) are not true. Now, Neg(R) is trivially equivalent to DISJ(Neg(Q_i), Neg(Q_j)), which is not true insofar as neither Neg(Q_i) nor Neg(Q_j) is true. Possibility 7: R is an existential generalization at least one of the instances of which is determined. At the nth step, at least one of the instances of R must occur, and of course be true. By hypothesis, the negations of such instances are not. Neg(R) in this case is trivially equivalent to a universal generalization, UG, the instances of which are the negations of the instances of R. Since at least one of the instances of R, say Q_i, is determined and occurs at the nth step in the determination of P, at least one of the instances of UG is not determined, and so UG is not determined. Consequently, Neg(R) is not determined, and so not true Possibility 8: R is a universal generalization each of the instances of which is true and occurs at the nth step. By inductive hypothesis, the negations of these instances are not true. Neg(R) is trivially equivalent to an existential generalization, EG, the instances of which are the negations of the instances of u. Since all of the instances of R are determined, none of the instances of EG is determined, and so EG is not determined. So, Neg(R) is not determined, and therefore not true. Possibility 9: R is analytically entailed by a determined proposition, Q_i. By hypothesis, Neg(Q_i) is not true, and so not determined. Now suppose that in fact Neg(R) is determined. Then since Neg(R) analytically entails Neg(Q_i), Neg(Q_j) would be determined as well, which it is not. Thus, Neg(R) is not determined.

The Inductive Step shows us that, under (FMT-G), given we are right about the Base Case, we know that if P is reached in any number of steps in any determination tree, then Neg(P) is not true. The complete proof therefore shows us that (FMT-G) sustains the principle that, where P is a truth-dependent truth, if P is true, then Neg(P) is not true. Given the definition of falsity for truth-dependent propositions in terms of the determination of the negation, we may infer that if a truth-dependent proposition is true, it is not false. And since, from the deflationary part of (FMT-G), we have it that if P is true, then P is not false, we may conclude that (FMT-G) sustains the general principle that for all P, if P is true, P is not false.

(C) is the claim that (FMT-G) yields the standard three-valued truth-tables. (C) is immediate from (FMT-G).

(D) is the claim that (FMT-G) entails, for every non-pathological proposition, the value of Tr for its corresponding instance of Excluded Middle. The following derivation is available to show that, given (FMT-G), it follows that for all non-pathological propositions P, the P-instance of Excluded Middle (EM(P)) is true. I use '$\rightarrow$' to express broad entailment (as a relation between propositions), and '$\leftrightarrow$' for broad equivalence. I use obvious abbreviations for 'truth-independent' and 'non-pathological'.

1. For all truth-ind. P, P$\leftrightarrow$Tr(P)   (FMT-G)
2. For all truth-ind. P, EM(P) is broadly necessary   Broad Logic
3. For all truth-ind. P, EM(P) is truth-ind.   Broad Logic
4. For all truth-ind. P, EM(P)$\leftrightarrow$Tr(EM(P))   1, 3

5.	For all P, Q, if P is broadly necessary, then $<P \leftrightarrow Q> \rightarrow P$	Broad Logic
6.	For all truth-ind. P, $<EM(P) \leftrightarrow (Tr(EM(P)))> \rightarrow (Tr(EM(P)))>$	2, 5
7.	For all truth-ind. P, if $EM(P) \leftrightarrow (Tr(EM(P))$, then $EM(P)$ is true	6, (PE), the principle of entailment)[19]
8.	For all truth-ind. P, $EM(P)$ is true	4, 7
9.	For all non-path., truth-dep. P, P is determined or $Neg(P)$ is determined	Def. of 'non-path'
10.	For all non-path., truth-dep. P, $EM(P)$ is determined	9, (Determination)
11.	For all truth-dep. P, P is true iff P is determined	FMT-G
12.	For all non-path., truth-dep. P, $EM(P)$ is true	10, 11
13.	For all non-path. P, $EM(P)$ is true	8, 12

(E) is the claim that (FMT-G) broadly entails principles of the attachment of truth/falsity, restricted to non-pathological propositions.

The demonstration consists of two simple conditional proofs. Suppose we have a non-pathological P. We show, first, that if P is true, $Tr(P)$ is true. Suppose P is true. We employ clause (ii) of (Determination) to conclude that $Tr(P)$ is true. Next we show that if $Neg(P)$ is true, then $Fls(P)$ is true. Suppose $Neg(P)$ is true. Clause (iii) of (Determination) assures us that $Fls(P)$ is true.

(F) is the claim that (FMT-G) sustains detachment principles for truth and falsity. First truth. Suppose $Tr(P)$ is true. If P is truth-independent, P is true by the deflationary theory of truth-independent truth. If it is truth-dependent, clause (ii) of (Determination) assures us that P is true. Now falsity. Suppose $Fls(P)$ is true. If P is truth-independent, $Neg(P)$ is true by the deflationary theory of truth-independent truth. If it is truth-dependent, we use clause (iii) of (Determination) to conclude that $Neg(P)$ is true.

(F) is of further interest. Attending to it, we see that (FMT-G) imposes a restriction on the intuitive linkages between truth and belief and truth and assertions. The intuitive link with assertion is well explained by Kripke (1975).

> We wish to capture an intuition of somewhat the following kind. Suppose we are explaining the word 'true' to someone who does not yet understand it. We may say that we are entitled to assert (or deny) of any sentence that it is true *precisely under* the circumstances when we can assert (or deny) the sentence itself. (Kripke 1975, p. 701) (My emphasis)

Kripke speaks of sentences, but the intuition extends to propositions. (FMT-G) in effect tells us to believe (assert) that liars are not true—and so to believe (and assert) with respect to any liar L we identify that it is not true; but it also tells us *not* to believe (and assert) with respect to any liar L we identify that it is *true* that it is not

---

[19] PE, again, is

If $<p>$ entails $<q>$, then if p, then q

true. In fact, (FMT-G) instructs us to believe just the opposite: with respect to any liar L we identify, we are told to believe that it is not true that L is not true, and what is more, we are told to believe that it is not true that it is not true that L is not true, *etc.* In other words for L we are told to believe (if we should ever broach the issue) each proposition in the series:

<L is not true>
<<L is not true> is not true>
<<<L is not true> is not true> is not true>
...

For no P are we told to believe both P and that P is false, but we are told to believe for pathological P both that P is not true and that it is not true that P is not true. This seems an odd, if not an outright unacceptable, instruction. I go some distance toward justifying it in the final section of this chapter.

(G) claims that (FMT-G) entails that every value of the forms <<p> is true iff p> and <<p> is false iff not-p> for a non-pathological argument is true. What goes for the equivalence form for truth goes for the form for falsity, and so I will focus only on the form for truth.

1.	For all non-path. P, either P is true or P is false	(FMT-G) From (A)
2.	For all non-path. P, if P is true, then Tr(P) is true	Attachment
3.	For all non-path. P, if P is true and Tr(P) is true, then IFF(P, Tr(P)) is true[20]	(FMT-G)
4.	For all non-path. P, if P is false, then Neg(P) is true.	(FMT-G)
5.	For all non-path. P, if P is false and Neg(P) is true, then IFF(Neg(P), Neg-Tr(P)) is true	(FMT-G)
6	For all non-path. P, if P is not true, then IFF(P, Tr(P)) is true	1, 5
7	For all non-path. P, IFF(P, Tr(P)) is true	3, 6
8	For all non-path. P, the value of <<p> is true iff p> for argument P is true.	7

We have merely applied the principles of (Determination), treating biconditionals as analytically equivalent to the appropriate conjunctions of disjunctions.

(H) is the claim that (FMT-G) entails the principles:

(H1)   For all P, Tr(P) broadly entails P
(H2)   For all P, Fls(P) broadly entails Neg(P)

If we can show that (FMT-G) entails the (H1), we can infer it entails (H2), since (H2) is equivalent to (H1), given (B), according to which Tr(P) and Neg(Fls(P)) are broadly equivalent. We show (H1) by a schematic proof. Assume <p> is true. We use (FMT-G) to show that p. <p> is either truth-independent or truth-dependent. If <p> is truth-independent, the deflationary part of (FMT-G), in conjunction with (PE),

---

[20] IFF(P,Q) is trivially equivalent to DISJ(CONJ(P,Q), CONJ(Neg(P), Neg(Q))), and so it is determined iff the latter is.

our principle of entailment, assures us that p. If <p> is truth-dependent, then it is determined, and has at least one determination tree. Given the deflationary part of (FMT-G), we know if there are truth-independent propositions <q_1>, ..., <q_n> at the tips, then q_1&...&q_n. We must show that p. We use an inductive proof on the number of steps in a determination tree of <p>.

The Base Case: the propositions occurring at the first step in a determination tree of <p>. Consider any such proposition <r>. Possibility 1: <r>=Neg-Tr(o) or Neg-Fls(o) for an o that neither is nor expresses a proposition. Parts III and IV of (FMT-G) then assures us that r, i.e., that o is not true (that o is not false). Possibility 2: <r>=Tr(<q_i>>) or Neg-Fls(<q_i>), where <q_i> is a truth-independent truth. This immediately assures us that r, for it assures us, by the deflationary part of (FMT-G), that <q_i> is true (and that it is not false). Possibility 3: <r>=Fls(<q_i>) or Neg-Tr(<q_i>). Same as in Possibility 2, *mutatis mutandis*. Possibility 4: <r>=Tr(x) or Neg-Fls(x) for an x that expresses a truth-independent truth. Part III of (FMT-G) immediately assures us that r, i.e., that x is true (that x is not false). Possibility 5: <r>=Fls(x) or Neg-Tr(x) for an x that expresses a proposition the negation of which is a truth-independent truth. Same as in Possibility 4, *mutatis mutandis*. Possibility 6: <r>=DISJ(<q_i>, Q>) for truth-independent <q_i> and some Q. Given that q_i, we know that r, where <r> is any disjunction containing <q_i> as a disjunct. Possibility 7: <r>=CONJ(<q_i>, <q_j>) for truth-independent <q_i> and <q_j>. Same as in Possibility 6, *mutatis mutandis*.

So by the Base Case, we know that if the determination of <p> consists of only one step, then p.

The Inductive Step: we assume that in any determination tree for <p>, where <q_i> occurs at the nth step, then q_i, and we show that, where <r> occurs at the n+1-th step, then r. Here there are nine possibilities. Possibility 1: <r>=Tr(<q_i>) or Neg-Fls(<q_i>). <q_i>, which occurs at the nth step in the determination of <p>, is then true and not false. Thus, r. Possibility 2: <r>=Fls(<q_i>) or Neg-Tr(<q_i>). Same as in Possibility 1, *mutatis mutandis*. Possibility 3: <r>=Tr(x) or Neg-Fls(x) for an x that expresses a truth-dependent truth, <q_i>, where <q_i> occurs at the nth step. Then by Part III of (FMT-G), x is true and not false, which is to say that r. Possibility 4: <r>=Fls(x) or Neg-Tr(x) for an x that expresses a truth-independent proposition the negation of which occurs at the nth step and is true. Same as in Possibility 3, *mutatis mutandis*. Possibility 5: <r>=DISJ(<q_i>, Q), where <q_i> is a truth-dependent truth occurring at the nth step. Then, by inductive hypothesis, q_i. Therefore, r. Possibility 6: <r>=CONJ(<q_i>, <q_j>), where <q_i> and <q_j> are truth-dependent truths occurring at the nth step. Same as in Possibility 5, *mutatis mutandis*. Possibility 7: <r> is an existential generalization with a true instance <q_i>, occurring at the nth step. Then, by inductive hypothesis, q_i. But then r, since for any x, where x is F, there is an x that is F. Possibility 8: <r> is a universal generalization the instances of which are the truth-dependent truths <q_i>, ..., <q_n>, occurring at the nth step. Then q_i&..., &q_n. And therefore, r, since for any x_1, ..., x_n, if x_1 is F, and if x_1, ..., x_n are all the things there are, then for all y, Fy. Finally, Possibility 9: <r> is analytically entailed by $<q_i>$ where $<q_i>$ is a truth-dependent truth occurring at the nth step. Then q_i, and so r, by the principle of entailment, (PE).

The Inductive Case assures us that if our treatment of the Base Case is correct, (H1) holds for any and all propositions in any determination tree of $<p>$, including $<p>$ itself. Thus, we have it that for all truth-dependent $<p>$, if $<p>$ is true, then p. Since this has been shown without the importation of any non-necessary facts, we may generalize to reach the conclusion that for all P, $Tr(P) => P$.

IV. A Dilemma?

(F) reveals a counter-intuitive consequence of (FMT-G). Lurking behind the linkages between truth and belief and truth and assertion is a dilemma waiting in the wings for anyone who attempts to give a general account of truth. It concerns the *answers* accounts of truth give for questions about whether liars are true or false. We seek an account of truth that will not merely declare liars neither true nor false, but will supply a general basis for such a declaration; thus, we seek an account that specifies unitary conditions CT and CF such that a proposition is true iff it meets CT and false iff it meets CF, and that yields the result that liars meet neither CT nor CF and so are neither true nor false. Supposing we have such an account, we must ask, with respect to anything that fails to meet either of CT or CF, whether it is *true* that it so fails; and our account will need to deliver an answer of "yes" or "no", depending upon whether the proposition that asserts its failure meets CT.

Now for the dilemma. Suppose we have a strengthened liar L. We ask: is it true that L fails to meet both CT and CF? If our account answers "no," we seem to have a right to protest, for since L doesn't meet either of these, it ought to be *true* that this is so. (Truth attaches.) But if our account answers "yes", telling us that it is *true* that L meets neither CT nor CF, we are faced with rather bleak alternatives: contradiction or repudiation of the principle of the transference of truth under analytic entailment, that if P analytically entails Q, then if P is true, Q is true. Why would we be forced to choose between acceptance of contradiction and abandonment of belief in the principle about analytic entailment? Suppose L = <The F is not true>, so that the F = L. And suppose our account tells us that the proposition <<The F is not true> does not meet CT> is true. Our account assures us that the proposition with respect to L that it is true is analytically equivalent to the proposition with respect to L that it meets CT. Then, if we accept the principle about analytic entailment, our account will be *mis*leading us. It will be telling us that <<The F is not true> is not true> is *true*. Yet once we put this together with our information about the identity of the F, we find ourselves concluding that the F is true! Thus, we find ourselves concluding that the F is both true and not true. The only path of escape is thus to reject the principle about analytic entailment at least in its unrestricted form.

This dilemma is closely related to our discussion of the simple account of determination in terms of broad entailment. The simple account falters because it commits its adherents to impalement on the second horn of our dilemma. Our account spares us from impalement on the second horn, given the last clause of

(Determination), which builds into the account the principle about analytic entailment. Does it therefore impale on the first horn? It does require acceptance of it, but does acceptance constitute *impalement*?

The principal danger attaching to the acceptance of the first horn is that it might prevent one from counting true *any* propositions that attribute CT or CF. Denying the truth of either

<<<Snow is white> is true> meets CT>

<<<Snow is green> is true> meets CF>

is intolerable. For, given our claim that truth-dependent propositions are true iff they meet CT, these denials would commit us, respectively, to denying the truth of the obvious truths

<<<Snow is white> is true> is true>

<<<Snow is green> is true> is false>

which is totally unacceptable.

However, if an account could be at once *selective* in its declarations concerning what meets (and fails to meet) CT (CF) and *principled* in its selectivity, acceptance of the first horn would not be impalement. The key question for any account of truth requiring acceptance of the first horn is whether the account sustains the following principles, with the translations for (FMT-G) given parenthetically:

(P1)   For any non-path., truth-dep. proposition P, P meets CT iff <P meets CT> meets CT.
(For any non-path., truth-dep. proposition P, P is determined iff Det(P) is determined.)

(P2)   For any non-path., truth-dep. proposition P, P meets CF iff <P meets CF> meets CT
(For any non-path., truth-dep. proposition P, Neg(P) is determined iff Det(Neg(P)) is determined.)

(P3)   For any path. proposition P, neither <P meets CT> nor <P meets CF> meets either CT or CF.
(For any path. proposition P, neither Det(P) nor Det(Neg(P)) are determined.)

If it does, we need not fear that our account will tell us that <<Snow is white> is true> is true> is not true. (FMT-G) clearly satisfies these principles. For suppose (FMT-G) is correct. Then for all truth-dependent P, Det(P) is analytically equivalent to Tr(P). Now suppose P is non-pathological. If P is determined, then by clause (ii) of (Determination), Tr(P) is determined. By clause (x), Det(P) is determined. If P is not determined, then P is not true, but false, and so Tr(P) is false, and so not true. But then Det(P) is also false, and so not true. (P2), under (FMT-G), is equivalent to (P1), and so our demonstration of (P1) demonstrates (P2) as well. Suppose now that

The Liar Paradox

P is pathological. Then P is not determined. So P is not true, and $Tr(P)$ is not determined. Thus, $Det(P)$ is not determined. Nor is $Neg(P)$, for since $Neg(P)$ is not true, $Tr(Neg(P))$ is not determined, resulting in $Det(Neg(P))$ being undetermined.

We may conclude that (FMT-G) leaves us unimpaled. Perhaps a better way to put it is this: there is really no dilemma of the kind we feared; there are two alternatives, one of which is acceptable. Admittedly, though, we abandon the powerful intuition connecting truth and assertion (belief) that forms the intuitive basis for Kripke's (1975) treatment of the liar-like pathologies. So, I will conclude with a discussion of the merits of my account as against Kripke's.

V. COMPARISON WITH KRIPKE'S ACCOUNT

Kripke introduces a semantic apparatus designed so as to count sentential liars as neither true nor false. (For a detailed and clear description of this apparatus, see Kirkham (1992, pp. 282-294)). For our purposes, we may describe Kripke's apparatus in application to an interpreted finite language L, with a nonempty domain D, where L is rich enough to express its own syntax and contains some coding scheme sufficient to provide codes for elements of D. Its variables range over D and its primitive predicates are totally defined by sets of n-tuples of objects in D.

We begin by specifying an extended language L_1 just like L with the sole addition being a pair of predicates left totally undefined, 'true' and 'false'. Now we give rules for extending any language L_i in the construction to form a language L_{i+1}. L_{i+1} assigns the same extensions and anti-extensions to all predicates other than 'true' and 'false' as L_i; L_{i+1} assigns to 'true' as its extension (and 'false' as its anti-extension) the union of the extension of 'true' under L_i and the set {Sentence $S \in L_i$: S = $\lceil \Phi \alpha \rceil$ and α denotes some d in the extension of Φ under L_i}; and L_{i+1} assigns to false as its extension (and true as its anti-extension) the set that is the union of the extension of false under L_i and the set {Sentence $S \in L_i$: S = $\lceil \Phi \alpha \rceil$ and α denotes some d in the anti-extension of Φ under L_i}.

This procedure can be specified inductively and can be expanded to permit assignment of truth-values to molecular and quantified sentences. (Again, see Kirkham 1992, pp. 284-5 for a clear account.) As one ascends the hierarchy of languages, the extensions and anti-extensions of predicates other than 'true' and 'false' (and predicates defined in their terms) remain unchanged. Since the stock of sentences in the language is finite, there will be some language in the hierarchy such that application of the specified rules to the language will yield that very same language. Such a language is a *fixed point*. 'True' and 'false', as interpreted in this language, are truth and falsity predicates. A sentence is then counted true (relative to the hierarchy of languages in question) iff it is counted an element of the extension of 'true' at the fixed point relative to the hierarchy, false iff it is counted an element of the extension of 'false' at the fixed point.[21]

---

[21] Kripke points out that there are different hierarchies of languages which conform to the rules he gives for extending languages and which agree with respect to the interpretation of all names and predicates other than 'true' and 'false'. Corresponding to each such hierarchy is

Kripke's construction process mirrors the supervenience of facts that involve sentential truth and falsity upon facts that do not. The process begins with the assignment of non-empty extensions and anti-extensions to predicates not involving 'true' or 'false'. This parallels the primacy, under my account, of the truth-independent facts. The first language in a Kripkean hierarchy, given the simple constraints, determines all the higher ones. These simple constraints parallel the principles of determination at work in my account.

Kripke's apparatus therefore seems to me to be anything but *ad hoc*, contrary to the claims of some critics. Kirkham, for example, charges that

> Kripke's solution is no more and no less ad hoc than is Russell's or Tarski's. He has no independent reasons, other than to solve the paradox, for placing the restrictions he does on what can and cannot have a truth value. (1992, pp. 291-2)

Kirkham goes on to say that the *ad hoc* element has been pushed to a deeper level in Kripke's account than it has in other solutions to the paradox, in that Kripke provides a general apparatus for counting the liar and its cousins as lacking in truth value. Against this, use of the apparatus has a strong philosophical justification in the supervenient nature of sentential truth.

Now for the key difference between my account and Kripke's. Kripke is motivated in large part by a conviction that there is a universal link between truth and assertion of the kind we discussed earlier. This link corresponds to rules for asserting truth and falsity of sentences S one understands

(Assertion rules)

One is entitled to assert of S that it is true iff one is entitled to assert S

One is entitled to assert of S that it is false iff one is entitled to deny S

One is entitled to assert of S that it is F iff one is entitled to deny of S that it is not-F

One is entitled to assert of S that it is false iff one is entitled to deny of S that it is true

One is entitled to deny S iff one is entitled to assert its negation.

(Here I extrapolate from Kripke's text (Kripke 1975, p. 701).) I will argue that an unflinching commitment to the Assertion rules forces one to make some implausible claims about liars, a conclusion that I believe Kripke himself implicitly accepts in his essay.

---

a fixed point. Thus, in place of L_1 above, one might substitute a language that differs from L_1 only in the inclusion of 'This sentence is true' in the extension of 'true' and the anti-extension of 'false'. The fixed point of the hierarchy described above is uniquely important, though, in that it is a *minimal* fixed point. This formal uniqueness is matched by an intuitive uniqueness to be described in the succeeding paragraph.

Affirming the Assertion rules guarantees that one is not entitled to assert of known liars that they are untrue. Here is why. Suppose one were entitled to assert of a liar sentence L that is untrue. Then one would be entitled to deny that L is true and so assert that it is false. But then one would be entitled to deny 'L is not false' and so assert 'L is false'. This would lead to an entitlement to assert that 'L is false' is true. And finally, since L = 'L is false' and one knows this, we would arrive at an entitlement to assert that L is true.

The alternative is to give up the Assertion rules, insist upon a distinction between asserting untruth and asserting falsity (of sentences), and permit the assertion of untruth to liars, even if this means also permitting the assertion of liars. (In the case of the strengthened liar, 'This sentence is not true', one would be entitled to assert both the sentence itself and the sentence attributing untruth to it.)

I recommend the second option. But first the vices of the first. Employing Kripke's inductive process, we seem to arrive at the conclusion that, because the liars are not in the extension of 'true' at any fixed point, they are not true. This conclusion appears to be confirmed by Kripke (1975, p. 714). For him, we are to deny truth—*i.e.*, the ordinary notion of truth—to liars.[22] But if we are to conclude that liars are untrue, why can't we assert it? And if we *can* assert it, the Assertion rules must go.

Now the virtues—the limited virtues—of the latter option. The best philosophical justifier for Kripke's account, I submit, is the claim that truth is supervenient, not the claim that truth is universally linked to assertion. Giving up this universal link does not mean allowing the assertion of what is believed false, only of certain propositions one believes to be untrue. The cost of this approach, however, is easily underestimated using the abstract language of "Assertion rules" and "links between truth and assertion." One need only consider a schematic question to remind ourselves:

> How can one be justified in asserting that p without being justified in asserting that it is true that p? (or that $<p>$ is true?)

---

[22] Kripke addresses these concerns in a well-known passage:

> ...the sense in which we can say, in natural language, that a Liar sentence is not true must be thought of as associated with some later stage in the development of natural language, one in which speakers reflect on the generation process leading to the...fixed point. It is not itself a part of that process. The necessity to ascend to a metalanguage may be one of the weaknesses of the present theory. The ghost of the Tarski hierarchy is still with us. (Kripke 1975, p. 714)

We cannot say using any fixed point language that a liar is untrue in the sense that the sentence 'L is not true', where 'L' in the language names a liar, is neither in the extension nor the anti-extension of 'true' ('false'). It is not interpreted.

In the metaphysical picture I have presented, there is no correlate of the distinction between object language and metalanguage. There simply is the determination of facts by the truth-independent facts. Liars are not determined, nor are their negations.

Theoretical development of the supervenient character of truth may go some distance toward an answer. My fear is that, past and future theoretical innovations notwithstanding, the question may disdain an answer, as do all rhetorical questions. My hope is that the rhetoric will lose its hold when the schematic 'that p' gives way to a pathological instantiation. I am encouraged when I ask myself:

> Granted that A = 'A is not true', how can one be justified in asserting that A is not true but not justified in asserting that it is *true* that A is not true?

Yet even if intuition permits only a rhetorical reading, we know the dangers that await those who follow their intuitions lead. To paradox! A sacrifice in intuition, albeit as minimal as possible, may be just what is required.

Perhaps more significantly, there is a more basic, if difficult to formulate, principle of assertion which could be used to justify the violation of Kripke's Assertion rules. The basic thought is that what can be justifiably believed can be justifiably asserted. This requires modification, however, due to certain pragmatic paradoxes. One may of course be justified in *believing* that one is not speaking, but this will not give one a justification for *asserting* that one is not speaking. By asserting that one is not speaking, one makes false what one justifiably believes. More broadly, if one is justified in believing P and if P entails that one does not assert it, then one is not justified in asserting it. So we will have to add a proviso to our permission rule regarding belief and assertion to this effect. But this proviso alone will not suffice. Gary Gates points out to me that where P = <I'm not entitled to assert P>, the permission rule, even given the former proviso, would grant me license to assert P, which intuitively it shouldn't do. Nor does it seem that merely adding a proviso requiring that P not entail that one is not entitled to assert P would suffice. For waiting in the works are propositions P_1 = <I'm not entitled to assert that I'm entitled to assert P_1>,..., P_n = <I'm not entitled to assert that...I'm entitled to assert P_n>,..., each of which I would seem to be justified in believing but not asserting. I hope the following stop-gap measure, however, will suffice to stave off further objections:

> If one is justified in believing that p and <p> is not about assertion or entitled assertion, then one is justified in asserting that p.

This principle certainly cannot be transformed into a principle of necessary and sufficient conditions. But if it is acceptable, we have what we need: a justification for thinking that one is justified in asserting that a liar is untrue.

Yet even if the sort of view of truth I've outlined is acceptable, further liar-like paradoxes involving justified belief and justified assertion seem to lay in waiting. For example, given the intuitive principles:

(J1) If one is justified in believing that one is not justified in believing that p, then one is not justified in believing that p.

(J2) If one is not justified in believing that one is not justified in believing that p, then one is justified in believing that p.

we have a paradox of justified belief, as follows. Let proposition $L = <-J(L)>$, *i.e.*, = $<$I am not justified in believing L$>$. (All this could be reformulated in terms of an indirect liar $L^* = <$I am not justified in believing the $F>$, where $L^* =$ the F.)

1. $L = <-J(L)>$ — Assm.
2. $J(L) \lor -J(L)$ — Assm.
3. $J(L)$ — Assm for Cond. Pf.
4. $J(<-J(L)>)$ — 1, 3
5. $-J(L)$ — 4, J1
6. $J(L) \to -J(L)$ — 3-5, Cond. Pf.|
7. $-J(L)$ — Assm. for Cond. Pf.
8. $-J(<-J(L)>)$ — 1, 7
9. $J(L)$ — 8, J2
10. $-J(L) \to J(L)$ — 7-9, Cond. Pf.
11. $J(L) \leftrightarrow -J(L)$ — 6, 10.

There is room for hope that J2 is unacceptable as it stands. In any case, we are threatened with a paradox of justified belief similar in certain ways to that of the liar.

I close with a pair of speculative questions, the consideration of which moves me to guarded optimism. Might the same trouble-making phenomena at the root of the liar pathologies also be at the root of the paradox of justified belief just discussed? Might the notion of grounding—grounding of truth, grounding of justification—hold the key to the solution of both supposed paradoxes?

Bibliography

Ackerman, F. (1995) How does Ontology Supervene on What There Is? In Savellos *et. al.* (1995), pp. 264-72.
Allaire, E. (1976) Ontologically Speaking Things Are. *Theoria*, 42, pp. 93-114.
Armstrong, D.M. (1978) *Universals and Scientific Realism*. New York: Cambridge University Press.
—— (1993) *Universals*. Boulder, CO: Westview Press.
Bealer, G. (1993) Universals. *Journal of Philosophy*, 90, pp. 5-31.
—— (1998) Propositions. *Mind*, 107, pp. 1-33.
Bennett, J. (1988) *Events and their Names*. Indianapolis: Hackett.
Bigelow, J. (1988) *The Reality of Numbers* Oxford: Clarendon Press.
Boghossian, P. (1990) The Status of Content. *The Philosophical Review*, 99, pp. 157-84.
Brand, M. and Walton, D., eds. (1976) *Action Theory*. Dordrecht, Reidel.
Butler, R. J., ed. (1962) *Analytical Philosophy*, 1st series. Oxford: Basil Blackwell.
Cartwright, R. (1962) Propositions. In R. J. Butler (1962), pp. 81-103.
—— (1987a) A Neglected Theory of Truth. In Cartwright (1987b), pp. 71-93.
—— (1987b) *Philosophical Papers*. Cambridge, MA: MIT.
Chalmers, D. (1996) *The Conscious Mind*. New York: Oxford.
Chisholm, R. (1996). *A Realist Theory of Categories*. New York: Cambridge University Press.
Davidson, D. (1996) The Folly of Trying to Define Truth. *Journal of Philosophy* 93, pp. 263-78.
—— (1986) A Coherence Theory of Truth and Knowledge. In LePore (1986), pp. 307-319.
—— (1990) The Structure and Content of Truth. *Journal of Philosophy*, 87, pp. 279-328.
Devitt, M. and Rey, G. (1991) Transcending Transcendentalism: A Response to Boghossian. *The Pacific Philosophical Quarterly*, 72, pp. 87-100.

Divers, J. and Miller, A. (1994) Why Expressivists about Value Should Not Love Minimalism about Truth. *Analysis*, 54, pp. 12-19.
Dummett, M. (1973) *Frege: Philosophy of Language*. Cambridge, MA: Harvard.
Dunn, M. and Gupta, A., eds. (1990) *Truth or Consequences*. Dordrecht: Kluwer.
Etchemendy, J. (1988) Tarski on Truth and Logical Consequence. *Journal of Symbolic Logic*, 53, pp. 51-79.
Field, H. (1994a) Disquotational Truth and Factually Defective Discourse. *The Philosophical Review*, 103, pp. 405-52.
—— (1994b) Deflationist Views of Meaning and Content. *Mind* 103, pp. 249-85.
Fox, J. (1987) Truthmaker. *Australasian Journal of Philosophy*, 65, pp. 188-207.
Frankfurt, H. (1971) Freedom of the Will and the Concept of a Person. *Journal of Philosophy* 68, pp. 5-20.
Grunderson, K., ed. (1975). *Minnesota Studies in the Philosophy of Science*, v. 7. Minneapolis, University of Minnesota Press.
Gupta, A. (1993a) Minimalism. *Philosophical Perspectives, 7, Language and Logic*, pp. 359-69.
—— (1993b) A Critique of Deflationism. *Philosophical Topics* 21, pp. 57-81.
Hale, B. (1987) *Abstract Objects*. New York: Basil Blackwell.
Heidelberger, H. (1968) The Indispensability of Truth. *American Philosophical Quarterly*, 5, 3, pp. 212-7.
Hochberg, H. (1978) *Thought, Fact, and Reference*. Minneapolis, MN: University of Minnesota Press.
Horwich, P. (1990) *Truth*. New York: Basil Blackwell.
—— (1993) Gibbard's Theory of Norms. *Philosophy and Public Affairs* 22, pp. 67-78.
—— (1995) Meaning, Use and Truth. *Mind* 104, pp. 355-68.
Jackson, F., Oppy, G., and Smith, M. (1994) Minimalism and Truth Aptness. *Mind* 103, pp. 287-302.
Kalderon, M.E. (1997) The Transparency of Truth. *Mind* 106, pp. 475-497.
Kim, J. (1976) Events as Property Exemplifications. In Brand and Walton (1976). Reprinted in Kim (1993c), pp. 33-52.
—— (1993a) Postscripts on Supervenience. In Kim (1993c), pp. 161-71.
—— (1993b) *Supervenience and Mind*. New York: Cambridge.
—— (1997) *Mind in a Physical World*. manuscript.
Kirkham, R.)1992) *Theories of Truth: A Critical Introduction*. Cambridge, MA: MIT Press.
Kovach, A. (1997) Deflationism and the Derivation Game. *Mind* 106, pp. 575-579.
Kripke, S. (1975) Outline of a Theory of Truth. *Journal of Philosophy*, 72, pp. 690-716.
—— (1980) *Naming and Necessity*. Cambridge, MA: Harvard.
LePore, E., ed. (1986) *Truth and Interpretation*. New York: Basil Blackwell.
Lewis, D. (1984) New Work for a Theory of Universals. *Australasian Journal of Philosophy*, 61, pp. 343-77.
—— (1986) *On the Plurality of Worlds*. New York: Basil Blackwell.
—— (1991) *Parts of Classes* New York: Basil Blackwell.
—— (1993) Mathematics is Megethology. *Philosophia Mathematica* 1, pp. 3-23.

—— (1975) Languages and Language. In Gunderson (1975). Reprinted in Lewis (1986), pp. 163-88.

—— (1986) *Philosophical Papers Volume 1*. New York: Oxford.

Lombard, L. (1986) *Events: A Metaphysical Study*. London: Routledge and Kegan Paul.

Mackie, J.L. (1977) *Ethics: Inventing Right and Wrong*. New York: Penguin.

McGrath, M. (1997). Weak Deflationism. *Mind*, 106, pp. 69-98.

—— (1997) Reply to Kovach. *Mind* 106, pp. 581-587.

—— (1998) The Concrete Modal Realist Challenge to Platonism. *Australasian Journal of Philosophy*, 76, 4, pp. 587-610.

Melia, J. (1995) On What There's Not. *Analysis*, 55, pp. 223-9.

Mellor, D.H. (1991) *Matters of Metaphysics*. New York: Cambridge University Press.

Mulligan, K., Simons, P., Smith, B. (1984) Truth-Makers. *Philosophy and Phenomenological Research*, 44, pp. 287-321.

Parret, H., ed. (1983) *On Believing*. New York: Walter de Gruyter.

Plantinga, A. (1973) *The Nature of Necessity*. New York: Oxford University Press.

—— (1987) Two Concepts of Modality. *Philosophical Perspectives*, 1, pp. 189-232.

Putnam, H. (1970) On Properties. In Rescher (1970). Reprinted in Putnam (1975), pp. 305-322. Page references are to the reprint.

—— (1975) *Philosophical Papers v.1: Mathematics, Matter and Method*. Second edition. New York: Cambridge.

—— (1981) *Reason, Truth, and History*. Cambridge: Cambridge University Press.

Quine, W.V. (1986) *Philosophy of Logic*. Second Edition. Englewood Cliffs: Prentice Hall.

—— (1992) *Pursuit of Truth*. Cambridge, MA: Harvard University Press.

Rescher, N. et. al., eds. (1970) *Essays in Honor of Carl G. Hempel*. Dordrecht: Reidel.

Restall, G. (1996) Truthmakers, Entailment, and Necessity. *Australasian Journal of Philosophy*, 74. pp. 331-40.

Rorty, R. (1979) *Philosophy and the Mirror of Nature*. Princeton, NJ: Princeton University Press.

Rosenthal, D., ed. (1991) *Nature of Mind*. New York: Oxford.

Savellos E., and Yalçin Ü., eds. (1995) *Supervenience: New Essays*. New York: Cambridge.

Schiffer, S. (1994) A Paradox of Meaning. *Nous* 28, pp. 279-324.

Sinnott-Armstrong, W., ed. (1995) *Modality, Morality, and Belief: Essays in Honor of Ruth Barcan Marcus*.

Smart, J.J.C. (1991) Sensations and Brain Processes. *Philosophical Review*, 68, pp. 141-56. Reprinted in Rosenthal (1991), pp. 169-76. Page references are to the reprint.

Smith, M. (1987) The Humean Theory of Motivation. *Mind*, pp. 36-61.

—— (1994) Why Expressivists about Value should Love Minimalism about Truth. *Analysis* 54, pp. 1-12.

Soames, S. (1995) T-Sentences. In Sinnott-Armstrong (1995) pp. 250-70.

Sosa, E. (1993) The Truth of Modest Realism. *Philosophical Issues*, 3, pp. 177-95.

—— (1983) Propositions and Indexical Attitudes. In Parret (1983), pp. 316-32.
Tye, M. (1981) Property Reduction and the Synonymy Principle of Property Identity. *Philosophical Studies* 40, pp. 177-85.
van Inwagen, P. (1986) Two Concepts of Possible Worlds. *Midwest Studies in Philosophy*, 11. Notre Dame, IN: University of Notre Dame Press, pp. 185-213.
Williams, M. (1988) Epistemological Realism and the Basis of Scepticism. *Mind* 94, pp. 415-39.
Wilson, K. (1990) Some Reflections on the Prosentential Theory of Truth. In Dunn and Gupta (1990), pp. 19-31.
Wright, C. (1992) *Truth and Objectivity*. Cambridge, MA: Harvard University Press.
—— (1983) *Frege's Conception of Numbers as Objects*. Aberdeen, Scotland: Aberdeen University Press.

Index

(AFT), 33
(E), 69
(FMT), 31
(FMT-G), 101-2
(PE), 31
(T), 73
Absurd confrontation objection, 52-4
Ackerman, Felicia, triviality challenge of, 13-16
Allaire, Edwin, 95n15
Analysis, 34
Analytic entailment, 111
Armstrong, D.M., 80, 87-8
Attributional priority thesis 7-8
Bealer, 29n9, 62
Bennett, Jonathan, 98
Bigelow, John, 97
Boghossian, Paul, 55
Bradley problem, 97
Concept horse, 7
Concept/property disinction, 16-24
Concete modal realism, 64, analysis of truth, 65
Correspondence theory, of propositional truth, 44-6
Counterpart theory, 78-80
Davidson, Donald, 30n13, 52-3

Deflationism, inadequacy of 34; contingency objection to, 35; strong, 39
Determination, 103; chains of, 105-7; 114
Devitt, Michael, 26n1
Direction of fit, 57
Disquotationalism, 26
Dummett, Michael, 5-6
Entailment, relation to truth, 43
Equivalence schemata, 27
Events, 44-6, 96-9, basic 96, 98-9
Explaining truth, 28
Explanation, 34, 63n7, 70
Field, Hartry, 35n23, 38, 47n8
Fox, John, 88, 95
Frege, Gottlob, 7
Gates, Gary, 132
Gupta, Anil, 27n5, 46n6, 47n9, 48
Hale, Bob, 5-6
Heidelberger, Herbert, 59n20
Higher-order quantification, 58-60
Internal vs. external relations, 76
Jackson, Frank, et. al., 56
Kalderan, Mark Eli, 58
Kim, Jaegwon, 19, 70, 97-8
Kirkham, Richard, 130
Kovach, Adam, 43
Kripke, Saul, 22-3, 118n17, 124, 129-31

Language: natural and abstract, 29 n10
Lewis, David, 29n10, chapter 4
Liar proposition, 188
Lombard, Lawrence, 98n23
Mackie, J.L., 5
Melia, Joseph, 4
Mixed sum duplication principle, 77
Moore, G.E., 40n30
Necessary connections, types I-III, 77
Non-factualism, 54-8
Pathology, liar-like, 119
Platonism, characterized 61-2, deflationist Platonism, 62-3
Predicatively involving truth, 150, 153-5
Primary/secondary intensions, 22-3
Primitivism, 40
Property deflationism, 27
Propositional forms 28-9.
Propositions, truth-free, 107; identificatory, 106; remainders, 107; truth-independent and truth-dependent, 108-110
Putnam, Hilary, 19-20, 27n3
Quine, W.V.O., 25-6
Reduction, 19-23
Restall, Greg, 90-3
Rey, Georges, 26n1
Robinson, Dennis, 97
Rorty, Richard, 57
Russell, Bertrand, 40n30
Schiffer, Stephen, 12
Searle, John, 57
Sosa, Ernest, on perspectivism, 17-8, 23-4; 30, 40n30, 72n17, 77n25
Stregthened liar proposition, 116-7
Structuralism, 82-5
Substitutional quantification, 28
Syntactic priority thesis, 7
Tropes, 93, 96,
Truthmaker Axiom, 89-90
Truthmaking, classical entailment account of, 89; appropriate entailment account of, 90; Weak Deflationist account of, 99-100
Truth-teller proposition, 118
Twin Earth cases, 18
Tye, Michael, 20-1
Universals, 80-1, 93, 96
Van Cleve, James, 59n20
Van Inwagen, Peter, 76, 78, 81
Weak Deflationism, 39, core idea of, 46, explanation of general facts within, 46-52; explanation of success, 48; explanation of instances of disquotation schema, 51-2
Williams, Michael, 25
Wright, Crispin, 4-5, 7, 55, 70

For Product Safety Concerns and Information please contact our EU
representative GPSR@taylorandfrancis.com
Taylor & Francis Verlag GmbH, Kaufingerstraße 24, 80331 München, Germany

www.ingramcontent.com/pod-product-compliance
Lightning Source LLC
Chambersburg PA
CBHW070403240426
43661CB00056B/2514